GOOD
WHOLESOME
COOKING

GOOD WHOLESOME COOKING

Pamela Westland

First published in 1986 by Octopus Books Limited
Grosvenor Street, London, England
© 1986 Hennerwood Publications Limited
ISBN 0 86273 331 6

Printed in England

CONTENTS

 # INTRODUCTION

Good, wholesome cooking – what a reassuring phrase that is! It conjures up visions of fresh, whole ingredients cooked in simple, down-to-earth ways. Food that is delicious and at the same time nutritious. Wholefood with none of the 'goodness' taken away from it, and with no unnecessary additives. Food that would contribute significantly to a healthy way of life for all the family. Food that our grandparents would have had respect for, and understood.

And yet following a wholefood programme isn't just a matter of turning back the clock and spurning many of the food products of the progressive technological age. It isn't quite as simple as that, for progress in dietary analysis has brought us a far better understanding of the foods we eat and the part they play in our day-to-day well-being and long-term health care. We know now, what caring cooks only a decade or so ago did not know: the vital importance of fibre in the diet, and the very real dangers of eating excess amounts of animal fats, sugars and salt.

Real food, wholefood When we refer to wholefood, basically we mean food that is grown or raised, produced rather than manufactured, and sold as close to its natural state as possible. It also means grains of all kinds complete with their all-important fibre content and the germ which is packed with so many nutrients, and a vitality-packed variety of fruit and vegetables, at their best when eaten fresh and – for even better nutrition – sometimes enjoyed raw. It means meat, poultry and fish too – for a wholefood diet is by no means limited to a vegetarian regime. But where red meats with a high fat content are concerned, it does mean enjoying them only in moderation.

The same applies to dairy produce and here there's a definite risk of confusing terminology. Just when we start getting the message that wholefood is good food, along comes the realisation that the whole animal fat content of milk, cheese, cream and yogurt, indulged in at will, is most certainly not good for us. Thus it is that skimmed and semi-skimmed milk (there are some really tasty brands on the market now) and low-fat hard and soft cheeses are interchangeable with and on some occasions preferable to the wholefood product.

As food technology has made giant advances in every direction, the number of components listed on manufactured foods has grown longer and ever more bewildering. Indeed, it is only a recent, and very important government requirement that food products must bear this detailed information.

Clearly by far the most satisfactory way of achieving nutritious and balanced meals without unwanted additives is to prepare and cook food at home, choosing ingredients which are as 'back to basic' as possible. Consider the difference in 'real food' terms between a home-made soup and a brand of canned soup. On the wholefood side,

compare our recipe for Tomato and watercress soup (page 17) – tomatoes, oatmeal, herbs, spices, chicken stock, lemon juice and salt – all familiar storecupboard ingredients – with the list on a canned vegetable soup. Apart from water and the vegetables there are flour, modified starch, skimmed milk, salt, vegetable oil, herbs, flavour enhancer (instead of more delicious herbs?), sodium glutamate, natural flavouring, artificial sweetener (saccharin) and colouring (tartrazine). I must stress that this is not to imply that all chemical food substitutes and all additives are harmful, it is simply to make the point that some prepared foods have come a very long way from the 'real thing'.

When every minute counts This new food revolution, the determination to improve our health by virtue of the food

we eat, has come upon us somewhat suddenly, and it takes time to realize the full implications. One thing it does not do – and this is a criticism levelled at healthy eating by many people – is this: it positively does not take more time to eat well and sensibly. Consider one of our examples above. It takes no longer to beat yogurt and whisk an egg white than it does to whip up the speediest of dessert toppings – and the enjoyment of the 'real food' will linger even longer.

Everyone is busy these days and so time is important and fast food, prepared in minutes and often eaten at the double, has practical appeal. But there's no conflict of interest here. Good, wholesome cooking does not need to be stood over and stirred over for hours, and fast food is not by any means necessarily junk food. Good wholesome cooking and fast food can be one and the same thing – and in many of the recipes that follow, they are just that.

Planning ahead can help to cut down preparation and cooking time. If you are soaking and cooking dried apricots for a dessert, for example, include enough to spare for one of those irresistible 'vitality' drinks that get the most sluggish of days off to a good start. When you are soaking and

cooking pulses for a casserole or a soup, add an extra handful so you have them on hand for an instant high-fibre salad, or to add to a clear soup or meat dish.

With an eye on the budget This brings us to another myth that is not always swiftly and convincingly dispelled – that healthy, wholefood cooking costs significantly more than prepared and processed foods. It is just as possible for people who eat basic, healthy foods to keep an eye on the family budget (and a firm hand on the purse-strings) as it is for those who eat nutritionally inferior, incomplete foods.

As you compare ingredients in the health food shops and on specialist counters you will find that some fruits and vegetables are described as 'organically grown' and some dried fruits as being 'natural'. This signifies the retailer's confidence that these foods have been grown in soil enriched with only organic waste products and without the aid of chemical pesticides or chemical fertilizers.

Foods grown without recourse to modern chemical preparations do cost a little more, to compensate the

growers for the lower yields they can expect from the acreage and, in many cases, for the cost of producing such foods on a comparatively small scale against massive competition. But things are changing, and as demand for food grown organically under natural conditions increases, the price gap should narrow.

Changing the emphasis on the proportion of the various foods you serve, cutting down on meat, oily fish and some dairy products whilst increasing the amounts of vegetables, pulses, grains and fruits, has a double purpose. Up goes the healthy aspect of the meal, and down goes the cost. Make a start by cutting the amount of red meat you serve by, say, 20% and making up the bulk of the meal with brown rice, other whole grains and green vegetables, roots, pulses and so forth and you will find that not only your well-being but your budget will reap the benefit.

The fibre story The importance of retaining the fibre in the foods we eat is one of the biggest stories to hit the dietary headlines in generations. Because fibre, which is present only in plant foods, does not contain any nutrients and cannot be digested, its value in health terms had been largely

overlooked. Dietary fibre is the 'support system' of all grains, cereals, vegetables and fruits, both the woody tissues (which are known as insoluble fibre) and the sticky gums (soluble fibre) which bind them together.

When wholewheat grains are milled to produce white flour, the bran (along with much of the germ) in the grains is processed out, leaving white flour which is capable of producing light, well-risen baked goods, but is woefully incomplete from the health point of view. Much the same applies when rice grains are processed. Oats, on the other hand, are not subject to the same type of health vandalism. No matter in what form you buy them – as rolled flakes, coarse, medium or fine oatmeal or oat flour – the whole grain is present, complete with the bran and the germ.

All whole grains, seeds, beans and peas (both fresh and dried), pippy fruits and dried fruits have a high proportion of fibre. In root vegetables and orchard fruits (which in general have less) much of the fibre is contained in the skin. This is why it is best to scrub potatoes and cook them in their jackets, and to wash and polish but not to peel apples.

Foods which have a high fibre content absorb liquid in the digestive tract like a sponge, become bulky and pass quickly and readily through the digestive system. Many of the diseases of the Western world have been identified as prevalent in populations who eat low-fibre diets – coronary heart disease, diverticular disease, bowel cancer and appendicitis among them – so, though the fibre story may make somewhat unpalatable reading, it is of great importance in the overall context of healthy eating.

Making a gradual change to a diet that contains more fibre is very simple. Always choose wholewheat bread and change to wholewheat flour, sometimes with the addition of oatmeal, for all your baking; include brown rice or other whole grains, wholewheat pasta, pulses or dried fruits in your menu at least once a day and you will be well on the way to the daily 30-35 grams of fibre recommended by dieticians.

The facts about fats Recent health reports have shown that at present 38% of the calories we consume are in the form of fat. With a high-fat intake now positively identified as a major cause of coronary heart disease, this is obviously more than is good for us. Current medical advice is that we should gradually reduce our fat intake until it represents no more than 30% of our total calorific intake, and that the fat we do consume should be equally and more beneficially divided between the three separate groups. These groups of fatty acids are, first, saturated fats, identified as the 'baddies' where health is concerned, and mainly of animal origin; at present they alone represent 20% of our calorific intake. Second, polyunsaturated fats, present in some measure in meat and oily fish, but mainly found in plants and seeds, and, third, monounsaturated fats, also mainly of plant origin.

Saturated fats are the ones that set hard at room temperature like the obvious rim of fat around a piece of meat, the block of butter or lard; in less obvious forms they are the 'hidden' fat that marbles meat and they are also present in milk, cream and soft cheeses. These are the fatty acids that can increase the amount of cholesterol in the

bloodstream and lead in time to blockage of the arteries.

Both groups of unsaturated fats are liquid at room temperature – and tend to come in bottles rather than in blocks. Polyunsaturates are now thought to be beneficial in lowering the cholesterol level of the blood, so whenever you choose cooking and salad oils, and indeed soft margarine, select those that are high in this group – soya, sunflower, safflower and corn oils, for example. Monounsaturates, found principally in olive oil, are thought to have no effect on the incidence of heart disease. The slightly cloudy, slightly thicker unrefined oils, known as cold-pressed or expeller-pressed, are the 'wholefood' ones, which give more character and flavour to cooked dishes and dressings. Refined oils, clearer and with the advantage of a longer shelf life, are the 'white flour' equivalents of the industry.

**Taking it with a pinch of salt** This is another aspect of healthy eating that has come under the spotlight recently. It might be thought that because salt is a natural mineral it has the go-ahead for unlimited consumption. But it is now realized that a large excess of sodium can contribute to high blood pressure, heart disease and brain haemorrhage. At present, as a nation, we are consuming 24 times our estimated daily minimum requirement.

Cutting down on salt used at table is an obvious first step. Simmer vegetables in stock flavoured with herbs and spices (a few parsley stalks, celery leaves, a bay leaf, a few peppercorns or a teaspoon of lemon juice) as an alternative to using salted water. Season egg dishes with turmeric or coriander and omit or cut down on the salt, add chopped fresh herbs to salad dressings and use them to garnish vegetables, use more herbs and spices in soups and meat casseroles and, by 'filling in' the flavour, you won't be accused of having forgotten something!

**Making the most of meat, poultry and game** Stir-fry beef in red sauce (page 37), Greek-style lamb (page 43), Casserole of pheasant with dried apricots (page 46) – there are some mouth-watering ways to make the most of meat, serving it as one of a well-balanced medley of ingredients rather than as the only attraction. Plan your menus to include the lowest-fat meats most often. These include chicken, turkey, rabbit and veal.

Remove the skin before cooking chicken, duck and other poultry – by far the greatest concentration of fat is in that area – or, if you do cook it, drain off all the fat from the pan and, when it comes to serving, make a determined effort to discard the skin. Cut away the visible fat from all cuts of meat and, when starting to make a casserole, dry-fry the meat in a good quality non-stick pan to draw off the hidden fat and discard it before going on with the dish.

Marinate poultry and meats in a little polyunsaturated oil, wine or vinegar and herbs; this will both flavour and tenderize the meat, and the marinade can be used as a stock or basting sauce. Stir-fry tender cuts of meat cut into thin shreds, they cook more quickly in a very little, very hot oil. That's not a contradiction; the meat will not absorb hot oil and, served with rice or noodles, a little goes a long way.

**Fishing for nutrients** Fish has a great deal to offer the healthy menu plan. It is rich in proteins, vitamins and minerals and relatively low in calories. A 100g (4oz) portion of white fish, such as cod, contains only 92 calories, compared with 120 for chicken. Trout (152 calories for the same weight), herrings (148), mackerel and salmon and all the other oily fish not surprisingly creep up the calorie scale, so put them into the 'little and not too often' category.

Marinate fish in tasty dressings, especially before grilling and baking, and introduce high-fibre foods into the dish in tasty ways. Jumbo oats as a topping for haddock casseroles (page 34), fresh green beans as a side dish to accompany Malay fish curry (page 34), wholewheat breadcrumbs and nuts as a stuffing for baked trout (page 52) – these are all ways to add variety of texture and flavour, and the all-important fibre content.

**Varying the vegetables** As meat steps back from the centre-stage position it has held for so long, so the balance tips and vegetables come into their own.

Filled vegetables, popular in Italian and Middle Eastern cooking, make a perfect main course. Fill vegetables like tomatoes, aubergines and peppers with a mixture of grains or breadcrumbs, a little meat or fish, sultanas, nuts, finely chopped root vegetables, pulses or what you will; grill or bake them with or without a cheese and yogurt sauce and you have an endless medley of nourishing ideas.

Nothing beats serving vegetables fresh from the garden – you can pick them when they are young and most tender and just minutes before you wish to serve them. If this is not an option, choose the freshest-looking vegetables you can find from a shop with a fast turnover. Tired-looking and wilting vegetables not only taste but a shadow of their former selves, they will have lost much of their nutritional value, for vitamins are lost on exposure to air and in water. Prepare vegetables just before you need them, wash and drain them well but never leave them to soak. Cook them as little as possible to preserve the maximum nutritional value.

Try steaming or baking carrot pennies and broccoli spears in foil parcels with a little stock and orange juice; courgettes and onion rings with sliced mushrooms in tomato juice; cauliflower florets and celery strips in soy-flavoured stock. Use a steamer (it saves fuel) to cook several vegetables on one heat source; that way, each one retains its identity. Stir-fry vegetables (partly cook tough roots first) with ginger, garlic and cashew nuts, making your selection with an eye on contrasting colours and shapes.

For the highest nutritional value of all – and I am still talking about irresistible combinations – serve vegetables raw as often as possible: crisp and crunchy crudités to go with dips and dunks, chilled green salads shining with freshness, and mixed salads introducing fresh and dried fruits, nuts, seeds and pulses – they all have taste appeal.

Refreshing ways with fruit Probably the most refreshing way of all to serve fruit is fresh – and what a time-saver that is! Polish apples till they shine and arrange them, and a few nuts or fresh dates, on a plate covered with evergreen leaves; arrange a dish of exotic-looking mango, watermelon and fresh fig slices, or add a few slices of kiwi fruit to spark up a dish of less expensive everyday fruits. Make fruit salad dressings with unsweetened fruit juices to replace calorie-laden sugar syrups, and add a stick of cinnamon or a clove to compensate for any loss of expected sweetness.

Capitalize on the concentrated sweetness (dietary fibre too) of dried fruits in all kinds of ways. Toss in a handful of sultanas or raisins when cooking apples, serve high-fibre dried apricots and blackberries with low-fibre sliced oranges, simmer apples and pears into dried apricot sauce.

Keep the dried fruit jars handy on baking day, too – there's plenty of scope for vine fruits – sultanas, raisins and currants – and orchard fruits in scones, teabreads, teacakes and fancy breads. More fibre, more flavour, less sugar is what today's baking is all about.

NOTES ON THE NUTRITIONAL INFORMATION GIVEN WITH THE RECIPES

The nutritional content of each dish is given at the top of the recipe. We have included values for energy, protein, fat, carbohydrate, sodium and dietary fibre. In order to make sense of the figures a little explanation is necessary.

Energy: Our requirement for energy varies greatly from person to person. One person's slimming diet might be that on which his neighbour would gain weight but the table below shows the approximate recommended daily allowances for healthy people at their ideal weight. Energy content of foods is often expressed in Calories – or nowadays Kilojoules (1 Calorie = 4.18 Kilojoules) so we have given both values with the recipe. Energy is obtained from the proteins, fats, carbohydrates and alcohol in our food.

Protein: Most people in the West obtain more than enough protein – there is no great advantage in eating much more than the values shown in the table – any excess is used to provide energy.

Fat: Again, most of us eat more than we need – currently it is suggested that we should aim to get about 30% of our energy from fat. As each gram of fat provides about 9 Calories, this works out roughly to the values given in the table. However children's fat intake is calculated as 35% energy.

Carbohydrate: Carbohydrate comes in many forms: simple, such as the sugars you put in tea or cakes or biscuits and complex – the starches found in grains, pulses, vegetables, etc. It is the latter group which people are now being encouraged to eat in larger quantities and it is suggested that at least 50% of our energy should come from such starchy carbohydrate with its dietary fibre intact. On the 'average' diet this would amount to around 250-300g per day – but remember, it is not possible to distinguish between the simple and complex carbohydrates in the recipes given here – take care with the ones which contain sugar or honey! The sugar in fruits – although 'simple' – is not so harmful as it is still associated with its dietary fibre and only released slowly into the body.

Sodium: Some authorities believe that most of us get more of this element than we need. It is mainly found as sodium chloride (salt) in foods but is present in other forms in such things as baking powder and bicarbonate of soda. Hints for cutting down on salt are given in the introduction. Currently 2000-3000mg of sodium a day is suggested as a suitable level to aim for (this is the equivalent to 5000-8000mg or 5-8 g of salt). The values given with each recipe do not include the salt added in cooking (1 teaspoon of salt = about 1600mg sodium) nor the salt in stock as this can vary a great deal.

Dietary fibre: In contrast to all the other items, here is something to increase rather than cut down on. Aim for 30-35g per day.

Remember: the nutritional information given is for these recipes only – the rest of the day's diet needs to be considered as well.

			Energy	Protein	Fat
			Calories	Megajoules*	(g)	(g)
RECOMMENDED	Moderately Active Man		2900	12.1	72	110
DAILY INTAKES	Moderately Active Woman		2200	9.2	54	80
OF ENERGY,	Boys	11-18 years	2700-2800	11.3-11.7	57-72	90
PROTEIN AND FAT	Girls	11-18 years	2100-2200	8.8-9.2	51-53	80
	Children	7-10 years	1900-2000	7.9-8.3	47-50	75-80
		*Megajoules= 1000 Kilojoules				

STARTERS, SOUPS AND SNACKS

Grilled Pepper and Mussel Salad

Per serving: 180 Calories, 750 Kilojoules, 6g Protein, 16g Fat, 4g Carbohydrate, 2g Fibre, 75mg Sodium

1 large red pepper
1 large green pepper
1 large yellow pepper (or use an extra green or red one)
4 tablespoons vegetable oil
2 teaspoons red wine vinegar
2 garlic cloves, peeled and finely chopped
3 tablespoons chopped fresh parsley
salt
freshly ground black pepper
1 × 100g (4oz) jar mussels in brine, washed, drained and dried
2 stalks tender celery, thinly sliced
curly endive or lettuce leaves (optional), to serve
sprigs of parsley, to garnish

Preparation time: 15 minutes
Cooking time: 20 minutes

1. Grill the peppers under medium heat for about 20 minutes, turning them frequently, until they are blackened and the skins have blistered.
2. Plunge the peppers into cold water, then drain them and pat them dry with paper towels. Using a small, sharp knife peel the skins from the peppers.
3. Halve the peppers, trim them and discard the seeds. Cut the peppers into 2.5cm (1 inch) wide slices.
4. Mix together the oil, vinegar, garlic and parsley and season the dressing with salt and pepper.
5. Toss the mussels in the dressing. Stir in the peppers and the chopped celery.
6. Line a serving dish with salad leaves if wished. Just before serving, spoon on the salad and garnish it with the sprigs of parsley.

Hazelnut and Vegetable Roll

Per serving: 190 Calories, 790 Kilojoules, , 12g Protein, 13g Fat, 7g Carbohydrate, 5g Fibre, 305mg Sodium

For a decorative way to serve the roll, pack it into 2 whole cored and seeded green peppers and wrap and chill them. Serve the peppers thinly sliced.

225g (8oz) low-fat soft cheese
75g (3oz) toasted hazelnuts, chopped
2 sticks tender celery, finely chopped
1 small green pepper, trimmed and finely chopped
2 spring onions, trimmed and finely chopped
1 medium carrot, finely grated
3 tablespoons chopped fresh parsley
salt
pinch of cayenne pepper
radicchio or endive leaves, to serve
2 large tomatoes, thinly sliced, to garnish
Coating:
3 tablespoons chopped fresh parsley
2 tablespoons toasted hazelnuts, chopped
2 tablespoons medium oatmeal

Preparation time: 15 minutes, plus chilling

1. In a bowl, mix together the cheese, nuts, celery, chopped green pepper, onions, carrot and 3 tablespoons parsley. Season with salt and cayenne pepper.
2. Beat the mixture well and shape it into a roll about 7.5cm (3 inches) in diameter. Wrap the roll in foil and chill it for 2-3 hours, or overnight.
3. Make the coating. Mix together the parsley, nuts and oatmeal. Roll the cheese mixture in the coating until it is evenly covered.
4. Line a serving dish with the salad leaves. Place the roll on them and garnish it with the tomato slices.

From the top: Grilled pepper and mussel salad; Hazelnut and vegetable roll

From the left: Wholewheat spaghetti with tuna sauce;
Wholewheat pizza with artichokes

Wholewheat Spaghetti with Tuna Sauce

Per serving: 540 Calories, 2250 Kilojoules, 26g Protein, 21g Fat,
62g Carbohydrate, 13g Fibre, 345mg Sodium
Per average serving of cheese: 120 Calories, 500 Kilojoules,
8g Protein, 10g Fat, 0 Carbohydrate, 0 Fibre, 185mg Sodium

275g (10oz) wholewheat spaghetti
salt
225g (8oz) mange-tout peas, topped and tailed
40g (1½oz) soft margarine
450g (1lb) small leeks, trimmed and thinly sliced
1 garlic clove, peeled and finely chopped
2 tablespoons wholewheat flour
300ml (½ pint) skimmed milk
300ml (½ pint) chicken stock
1 × 225g (8oz) can tuna fish in brine, drained and flaked
2 tablespoons snipped fresh chives
freshly ground black pepper
2 tablespoons chopped fresh parsley
sprigs of parsley, to garnish
grated low-fat hard cheese, to serve

Preparation time: 15 minutes
Cooking time: 40 minutes

1. Cook the spaghetti in a large saucepan of boiling salted water for 10-12 minutes, or until it is just tender. Drain into a colander, run hot water through it, drain again and return the spaghetti to the pan. Cover, and keep the pasta warm.
2. Meanwhile, partly cook the mange-tout peas by steaming them over boiling, salted water for about 8 minutes until they are almost tender.
3. Heat the margarine in a medium saucepan and fry the leeks and garlic over moderate heat for 5 minutes, stirring frequently. Lift out the leeks and set them aside.
4. Stir the flour into the margarine until it forms a smooth paste, then gradually pour on the milk and stock, stirring constantly. Stir the leeks, mange-tout peas, tuna fish and chives into the sauce, taste and season with salt and pepper. Simmer for 3 minutes.
5. Turn the spaghetti into a heated serving dish, pour on the sauce and toss it well, using 2 wooden spoons. Sprinkle on the chopped parsley garnish with the sprigs. Hand the cheese separately.

Wholewheat Pizza with Artichokes

Per serving: 380 Calories, 1590 Kilojoules, 16g Protein, 19g Fat, 39g Carbohydrate, 8g Fibre, 660mg Sodium

175g (6oz) wholewheat self-raising flour
salt
freshly ground black pepper
1 teaspoon grated lemon rind
50g (2oz) soft margarine
6 tablespoons plain unsweetened yogurt
Filling:
450g (1lb) tomatoes, skinned and chopped
1 medium onion, peeled and chopped
1 garlic clove, peeled and crushed
4 tablespoons chopped fresh mint
1 teaspoon lemon juice
1 × 400g (14oz) can artichoke hearts, drained, rinsed, dried and sliced
150g (5oz) Ricotta cheese, crumbled
100g (4oz) button mushrooms, thinly sliced
12 black olives, halved and stoned
1 tablespoon vegetable oil, for brushing
2 tablespoons grated Parmesan
sprig of mint, to garnish

Preparation time: 20 minutes
Cooking time: 50 minutes
Oven: 200°C, 400°F, Gas Mark 6

1. In a large bowl mix together the flour, salt, pepper and lemon rind. Mix in the margarine and yogurt and form the mixture into a ball. Knead the dough in the bowl until it is smooth. F Roll out the dough on a lightly-floured board and use it to line a 25cm (10 inch) greased flan ring placed on a greased baking sheet. F Prick the pizza base all over with a fork, line it with greaseproof paper and fill it with dried 'baking' beans.
2. Bake the pizza base in a preheated oven for 15 minutes, then remove the baking beans and paper. F
3. Make the filling while the pizza base is cooking. Put the tomatoes, onion, garlic, 2 tablespoons of the mint and the lemon juice into a small saucepan, season with salt and pepper, then bring the mixture to the boil, stirring occasionally. Simmer for 20 minutes, or until the sauce is like a thick paste. Taste and adjust the seasoning if necessary. Stir in the remaining mint.
4. Spread the tomato paste over the pizza base, then spread over the sliced artichoke hearts, reserving 4 slices for the top. Sprinkle on the Ricotta cheese and cover it with the mushroom slices. Arrange the reserved artichoke slices and the halved black olives in a pattern, and brush the top of the pizza with oil. F

5. Return to the oven and bake for 12 minutes. Sprinkle over the grated Parmesan and return the pizza to the oven for a further 2 minutes. Garnish with a sprig of mint and serve immediately.
F The unbaked pizza dough can be rolled out, packed in a polythene bag and frozen for up to 3 months. Add the topping and bake from frozen, allowing 25 minutes.
The partly cooked pizza base can be frozen for 2 months. Open-freeze the prepared pizza, then wrap with freezer film when firm and freeze for up to 1 month. Cook from frozen for 30-35 minutes.

Mushroom Pâté

Per serving: 145 Calories, 610 Kilojoules, 3g Protein, 9g Fat, 11g Carbohydrate, 3g Fibre, 15mg Sodium

If you have 1 or 2 small button mushrooms, they make an appropriate and decorative garnish. Slice them thinly through the stalk and cap and arrange 2 or 3 slices with the herb sprig on each portion.

2 tablespoons vegetable oil
1 medium onion, peeled and finely chopped
2 garlic cloves, peeled and crushed
225g (8oz) field mushrooms, peeled and chopped
175g (6oz) cottage cheese
50g (2oz) medium oatmeal
1 teaspoon soy sauce
3 tablespoons medium sherry
salt
freshly ground black pepper
2 tablespoons chopped fresh parsley
1 tablespoon snipped fresh chives
sprigs of parsley, to garnish

Preparation time: 15 minutes, plus chilling
Cooking time: 12 minutes

1. Heat the oil in a small saucepan and fry the onion over moderate heat for 3 minutes, stirring once or twice. Add the garlic and mushrooms, reduce the heat to low and cook for 7-8 minutes, stirring occasionally.
2. Lift out the vegetables with a draining spoon and put them in a blender with the cottage cheese, oatmeal, soy sauce and sherry. Blend until the mixture is smooth. Taste the pâté and season it to taste with salt and pepper.
3. Turn the mixture into a bowl and stir in the parsley and the snipped chives.
4. Spoon the pâté into 4 ramekin dishes, smooth the top and cover with film or foil. Chill for 2-3 hours, or overnight, before serving. A F Garnish with the parsley sprigs.
A The pâté can be kept in the refrigerator for 2 days.
F Overwrap with foil and freeze for up to 2 months. Thaw overnight in the refrigerator or for 2-3 hours at room temperature.

From the left: Golden soup; Green salad soup;
Apple and coriander soup

Golden Soup

Per serving: 195 Calories, 815 Kilojoules, 13g Protein, 2g Fat,
35g Carbohydrate, 16g Fibre, 280mg Sodium

175g (6oz) haricot beans, soaked overnight and drained
450g (1lb) carrots, sliced
1 large onion, peeled and sliced
1 litre (1¾ pints) chicken stock
1 bouquet garni
salt
freshly ground black pepper
pinch of cayenne pepper
4 tablespoons plain unsweetened yogurt
Croûtons:
2 large slices wholewheat bread
4 tablespoons chopped fresh parsley

Preparation time: 10 minutes, plus soaking
Cooking time: 1½ hours

1. Cook the beans in a large saucepan of boiling unsalted water for 30 minutes. Make sure that the water is fast-boiling for the first 15 minutes to kill any harmful toxins. Drain the beans.
2. Return the partly-cooked beans to the saucepan and add the carrots, onion, stock and the bouquet garni. Bring to the boil, cover the pan, and simmer for 45 minutes.
3. Using a draining spoon, lift out and reserve about 2 tablespoons of the beans. Discard the bouquet garni.
4. Liquidize the remaining vegetables and the stock in a blender. Alternatively, rub them through a sieve or work them through a vegetable mill.
5. Return the purée to the saucepan, season with salt, pepper and cayenne and stir in the yogurt. Reheat the soup gently and float the reserved beans on the top.
6. To make the croûtons, toast the bread on both sides and cut it into 1cm (½ inch) squares. Toss them at once, while they are still hot and moist, into the chopped parsley. Serve these low-fat croûtons separately.

1. Heat the margarine in a large saucepan and fry the onion over moderate heat for 3 minutes, stirring once or twice.
2. Add the lettuce, green pepper, spinach leaves and 2 tablespoons of the mint, stir well and simmer for 3 minutes. Pour on the stock, milk and lemon juice and bring to the boil. Cover and simmer for 15 minutes.
3. Liquidize the vegetables in a blender or work them in a vegetable mill to make a smooth purée.
4. Return the purée to the pan, season with salt, pepper and nutmeg and stir in the yogurt. Heat the soup gently, taste and adjust the seasoning if necessary.
5. Garnish the soup with the remaining mint, float a sprig on each bowl, and serve the pumpkin seeds separately.

Apple and Coriander Soup

Per serving: 185 Calories, 770 Kilojoules, 6g Protein, 6g Fat, 29g Carbohydrate, 6g Fibre, 215mg Sodium

25g (1oz) soft margarine
1 onion, peeled and sliced
1 garlic clove, peeled and chopped
2 teaspoons ground coriander
1 medium potato, peeled and roughly chopped
750g (1½ lb) cooking apples, peeled, cored and chopped
600ml (1 pint) chicken stock
300 ml (½ pint) buttermilk
salt
freshly ground black pepper
1 tablespoon lemon juice
2 tablespoons chopped fresh coriander or mint
<u>To garnish:</u>
50g (2oz) low-fat soft cheese
fresh sprigs of coriander or mint

Preparation time: 15 minutes
Cooking time: 30 minutes

1. Melt the margarine in a saucepan and fry the onion and garlic over moderate heat for 2 minutes. Stir in the ground coriander and cook for 1 minute, stirring.
2. Add the potato and apple, stir well and cook for 2-3 minutes. Pour on the stock, stirring all the time, and then the buttermilk. Season with salt and pepper.
3. Bring to the boil, cover the saucepan and simmer for 15 minutes. Stir in the lemon juice and chopped herb.
4. Liquidize the soup in a blender. Alternatively, rub it through a sieve or work it through a vegetable mill to make a smooth purée.
5. Reheat the soup gently. Taste, and adjust the seasoning if necessary. Pour the soup into individual bowls and garnish each one with a spoonful of soft cheese and a sprig of fresh coriander or mint.

Green Salad Soup

Per serving: 210 Calories, 880 Kilojoules, 13g Protein, 12g Fat, 14g Carbohydrate, 6g Fibre, 225mg Sodium

25g (1oz) soft margarine
1 medium onion, peeled and sliced
½ small lettuce, sliced
1 green pepper, cored, seeded and sliced
225g (8oz) spinach leaves
4 tablespoons chopped fresh mint, and sprigs to garnish
450ml (¾ pint) chicken stock
450ml (¾ pint) skimmed milk
2 teaspoons lemon juice
salt
freshly ground black pepper
large pinch of nutmeg
150ml (¼ pint) plain unsweetened yogurt
3-4 tablespoons pumpkin seeds, to serve

Preparation time: 15 minutes
Cooking time: 25 minutes

Rasan Soup

Per serving: **295** Calories, **1230** Kilojoules, **26g** Protein, **4g** Fat, **40g** Carbohydrate, **7g** Fibre, **500mg** Sodium

Grilled poppadoms and hot wholewheat pitta bread make tasty accompaniments to this spicy soup.

100g (4oz) yellow split peas, soaked overnight and drained
1 medium onion, peeled and finely chopped
2 sticks tender celery, thinly sliced
1 small leek, trimmed and thinly sliced
2 teaspoons grated lemon rind
3 tablespoons lemon juice
$\frac{1}{2}$ teaspoon ground turmeric
2 tablespoons medium oatmeal
1 litre ($1\frac{3}{4}$ pints) chicken stock
salt
freshly ground black pepper
4 tablespoons plain unsweetened yogurt (optional)
4 thin lemon slices, to garnish

Preparation time: 15 minutes
Cooking time: 55 minutes

1. Put the split peas, onion, celery, leek, lemon rind, lemon juice, turmeric and oatmeal into a saucepan, stir them together and pour on the stock. Bring to the boil, cover and simmer for 45 minutes.
2. Season with salt and pepper and simmer for 5 minutes.
3. Swirl the yogurt on top, if wished, and garnish the soup with the lemon slices. Serve hot.

Fish and Sweetcorn Chowder

Per serving: **250** Calories, **1050** Kilojoules, **23g** Protein, **4g** Fat, **34g** Carbohydrate, **5g** Fibre, **340mg** Sodium

350g (12oz) white fish fillet, such as coley or cod
450ml ($\frac{3}{4}$ pint) skimmed milk
1 bay leaf
4-6 peppercorns
4-6 parsley stalks
350g (12oz) potatoes, peeled and sliced
225g (8oz) frozen sweetcorn kernels
salt
15g ($\frac{1}{2}$oz) soft margarine
1 medium onion, peeled and sliced
2 teaspoons mustard powder
freshly ground black pepper
3 tablespoons chopped fresh parsley

Clockwise from top left: Fish and sweetcorn chowder; Tomato and watercress soup; Rasan soup

Preparation time: 15 minutes
Cooking time: 45 minutes

1. Put the fish into a frying pan with the milk, bay leaf, peppercorns and parsley stalks. Bring it slowly to the boil and poach for 10 minutes. Lift out the fish and, when it is cool enough to handle, flake the fish removing the skin and any bones. Strain and reserve the milk.
2. Cook the potatoes and sweetcorn kernels in boiling salted water for 15 minutes. Drain the vegetables and reserve 450ml ($\frac{3}{4}$ pint) of the liquid.
3. Melt the margarine in a large saucepan and fry the onion over moderate heat for 4 minutes, stirring once or twice. Stir in the mustard powder, then pour on the reserved milk and the vegetable liquid, stirring all the time. Add the flaked fish, the potatoes and sweetcorn, season with salt and pepper and stir in 2 tablespoons of the parsley. Simmer for 5 minutes until the fish and vegetables are warmed through.
4. Sprinkle on the remaining parsley. Serve hot, with small triangles of wholemeal toast.

1. Put the tomatoes into a medium saucepan over moderate heat and stir in the oatmeal and paprika. When the oatmeal is well blended, stir in the oregano and mint. Tie the bay leaves, mace, peppercorns, parsley and celery leaves into a piece of muslin and add them to the pan with the chicken stock. Stir well and bring the soup slowly to the boil, stirring constantly.

2. Cover the pan and simmer for 20 minutes. Discard the bag of flavourings. Put the tomatoes in a blender and liquidize them to make a smooth purée. Alternatively, rub them through a sieve or work in a vegetable mill.

3. Return the purée to the pan. Chop the watercress and stir it into the purée with the lemon juice and season with salt and pepper. Simmer for about 3 minutes until the watercress is just tender. Garnish the soup with the reserved celery leaves and serve hot.

Jerusalem Artichoke and Buttermilk Soup

Per serving: 100 Calories, 420 Kilojoules, 9g Protein, Trace Fat, 15g Carbohydrate, 1g Fibre, 235mg Sodium

450g (1lb) Jerusalem artichokes, peeled or scrubbed and roughly chopped
450g (1lb) potatoes, peeled and roughly chopped
1 large onion, peeled and sliced
300ml ($\frac{1}{2}$ pint) chicken stock
600ml (1 pint) buttermilk
2 bay leaves
1 blade of mace
4-6 parsley stalks
strip of thinly pared orange rind
3 tablespoons orange juice
salt
freshly ground black pepper
4 tablespoons plain unsweetened yogurt
2 tablespoons chopped fresh parsley, to garnish

Preparation time: 20 minutes
Cooking time: 35 minutes

1. Put the artichokes, potatoes and onion into a saucepan with the stock and buttermilk. Tie the bay leaves, mace, parsley stalks and orange rind into a piece of muslin and add them to the pan.

2. Bring the soup slowly to the boil, cover, and simmer for 20 minutes.

3. Discard the bundle of flavourings. Liquidize the soup in a blender or rub it through a sieve to make a purée.

4. Return the purée to the pan, stir in the orange juice and season with salt and pepper. Simmer for 3-4 minutes.

5. Swirl the yogurt over the soup, garnish with the parsley and serve hot.

Tomato and Watercress Soup

Per serving: 50 Calories, 210 Kilojoules, 3g Protein, 1g Fat, 9g Carbohydrate, 4g Fibre, 15mg Sodium

450g (1lb) tomatoes, skinned and chopped
2 tablespoons fine oatmeal
1 teaspoon paprika
1 teaspoon dried oregano
2 tablespoons chopped fresh mint
2 bay leaves
1 blade of mace
6 peppercorns
4-6 parsley stalks
2 tablespoons celery leaves, plus some for garnish
750ml (1$\frac{1}{4}$ pints) chicken stock
1 bunch watercress sprigs, trimmed
2 teaspoons lemon juice
salt
freshly ground black pepper

Preparation time: 15 minutes
Cooking time: 30 minutes

From the top: Potato and herb triangles; Walnut soda bread

Potato and Herb Triangles

Per triangle: 65 Calories, 270 Kilojoules, 8g Protein, 1g Fat, 7g Carbohydrate, 1g Fibre, 100mg Sodium

Potato triangles are good as a snack spread with low-fat soft cheese, or they can be served with soup.

Makes about 8 triangles
350g (12oz) potatoes, peeled
salt
freshly ground black pepper
2 tablespoons snipped fresh chives
2 tablespoons chopped fresh parsley
75g (3oz) wholewheat flour
a little milk (optional)
oil for brushing (optional)

Preparation time: 15 minutes
Cooking time: 35 minutes

1. Boil the potatoes in lightly salted water for 15-20 minutes until they are tender. Drain them.
2. Mash the potatoes well. If you have one, work them through a potato 'ricer'. This helps to lighten the mixture. Season the potatoes with salt and pepper and stir in the chives and parsley. Beat in the flour and add a little milk if the mixture is too dry – it should be able to hold its shape easily without breaking.
3. Form the mixture into a ball and knead the dough lightly until it is smooth and free from cracks. Roll it out on a lightly floured board to a thickness of 5mm ($\frac{1}{4}$ inch). Prick the surface of the dough all over with a fork and cut it into neat triangles.
4. Use a good quality non-stick frying pan or lightly brush a heavy-based frying pan with oil. Heat the pan over a moderate heat and cook the triangles, a few at a time, for 2-3 minutes on each side until they are golden brown.

Walnut Soda Bread

Per average slice: 215 Calories, 900 Kilojoules, 9g Protein, 5g Fat, 36g Carbohydrate, 5g Fibre, 300mg Sodium

Makes one 18cm (7 inch) round loaf
450g (1lb) wholewheat flour
2 teaspoons baking powder
1 teaspoon salt
1 tablespoon light muscovado sugar
75g (3oz) chopped walnuts
300ml ($\frac{1}{2}$ pint) plain unsweetened yogurt
water to mix
2 tablespoons milk
2 tablespoons cracked wheat

Preparation time: 15 minutes
Cooking time: 40 minutes
Oven: 190°C, 375°F, Gas Mark 5

1. Sift the flour, baking powder and salt into a mixing bowl and stir in the sugar and walnuts. Stir in the yogurt and sufficient water to make a firm dough.
2. Knead the dough lightly in the bowl until it is smooth and free from cracks.
3. Shape the dough into a round about 18cm (7 inches) in diameter and place it on a greased baking sheet. Mark the top into 4 segments. Brush the top with milk and sprinkle with the cracked wheat.
4. Bake the loaf in a preheated oven for 40 minutes, or until it is well risen and firm and sounds hollow when tapped underneath. Cool on a wire rack.

Oatmeal Bread Squares

Per square: 115 Calories, 485 Kilojoules, 4g Protein, 3g Fat, 20g Carbohydrate, 2g Fibre, 10mg Sodium

Makes 12 squares
100g (4oz) medium oatmeal
150ml ($\frac{1}{4}$ pint) skimmed milk, plus 2 tablespoons for brushing
175g (6oz) wholewheat self-raising flour
1 teaspoon baking powder
salt
freshly ground black pepper
4 tablespoons jumbo oats
1 tablespoon vegetable oil
2 tablespoons snipped fresh chives

Preparation time: 25 minutes
Cooking time: 25 minutes
Oven: 230°C, 450°F, Gas Mark 8

1. Soak the oatmeal in the milk for 15 minutes.
2. Sift the flour, baking powder, salt and pepper into a bowl and tip in the bran remaining in the sieve. Stir in 2 tablespoons of the jumbo oats, the oil and the chives.
3. Stir the dry ingredients into the soaked oatmeal and mix to a firm dough. Knead the dough until it is smooth and free from cracks.
4. Press the dough into a greased 23 × 18cm (9 × 7 inch) baking dish and mark the top into 12 squares. ⒡Brush the top with milk and sprinkle on the reserved jumbo oats.
5. Bake the bread in a preheated oven for 20–25 minutes until it is well risen and firm.
6. Stand the tin on a wire rack to cool slightly, then cut into the marked squares. Serve the bread slightly warm.
⒡Freeze the unbaked dough for 3 months and bake from frozen. Allow an extra 5-7 minutes cooking time, lowering the temperature to 190°C, 375°F, Gas Mark 5.

Spinach Pancakes

Per small pancake: 125 Calories, 520 Kilojoules, 8g Protein, 7g Fat, 6g Carbohydrate, 2g Fibre, 165mg Sodium

Makes about 8-12 pancakes
75g (3oz) wholewheat flour
salt
2 eggs
200ml (7fl oz) skimmed milk
1 tablespoon vegetable oil
175g (6oz) frozen leaf spinach, thawed and liquidized
freshly ground black pepper
pinch of grated nutmeg
oil for brushing
sprigs of parsley, to garnish
Filling:
2 tablespoons vegetable oil
1 small onion, peeled and chopped
2 green peppers, seeded, cored and chopped
40g (1½oz) low-fat hard cheese, grated
175g (6oz) Ricotta cheese
100g (4oz) low-fat cottage cheese, sieved
1 egg
2 tablespoons chopped fresh parsley
freshly ground black pepper
pinch of cayenne pepper
2 tablespoons low-fat hard cheese, grated

Preparation time: 45 minutes
Cooking time: 1 hour
Oven: 180°C, 350°F, Gas Mark 4

1. Sift the flour and salt into a mixing bowl and tip in the bran remaining in the sieve. Beat in the eggs. Gradually beat in the milk and the oil. Stir in the spinach purée and season with pepper and nutmeg.
2. To make a filling, heat the oil in a small saucepan and fry the chopped onion and green peppers over a moderate heat for 4 minutes, stirring once or twice. Lift out the vegetables with a draining spoon and toss them on paper towels to dry. In a medium bowl beat together the Ricotta and cottage cheese. Beat in the egg and stir in the vegetables and parsley. Season the mixture with pepper and cayenne and stir in the grated cheese.
3. Lightly brush a 13cm (5 inch) pancake pan or frying pan with oil and heat it over moderate heat. Pour in about 3 tablespoons of the batter, tilt the pan so that it covers the base evenly and cook for about 3 minutes, or until bubbles appear on the surface. Flip or toss the pancake and cook the other side for about 2 minutes until it begins to brown.
4. Slide the cooked pancake on to a heated plate, cover with foil and keep it warm while you cook all the remaining batter in the same way. Ⓕ
5. When all the pancakes are cooked, spread a little of the filling thinly over each one. Fold the pancakes in half, and then in half again, to make a wedge shape. Spoon the remaining filling into the opening.
6. Arrange the pancakes on a heated ovenproof dish. Sprinkle with grated cheese and garnish with parsley.
7. Heat the pancakes in a preheated oven for 15 minutes. Serve hot.
Ⓕ Leave the pancakes to cool, then layer with polythene and pack into a sealed container and freeze for 3 months. Thaw for 1 hour at room temperature.
Ⓜ Thaw in layers of 4 on Defrost for 2-4 minutes or until soft. Leave to stand for 5 minutes before serving.

Sage Dairy Bread

Per slice: 160 Calories, 670 Kilojoules, 8g Protein, 1g Fat, 32g Carbohydrate, 4g Fibre, 340mg Sodium

This loaf is best served on the day of baking

Makes one loaf
225g (8oz) wholewheat flour
225g (8oz) granary flour, plus extra for sprinkling
1 teaspoon salt
2 teaspoons baking powder
1 teaspoon bicarbonate of soda
100g (4oz) low-fat cottage cheese
1 tablespoon chopped fresh sage, or 1 teaspoon dried sage
1 teaspoon lemon juice
about 50-85ml (2-3fl oz) skimmed milk, plus extra for brushing

Preparation time: 15 minutes
Cooking time: 25 minutes
Oven: 220°C, 425°F, Gas Mark 7

1. Sift the flours, salt, baking powder and soda into a mixing bowl and tip in the bran remaining in the sieve. Stir in the cottage cheese and sage and sprinkle on the lemon juice. Pour on the milk, mixing all the time, adding just enough to make a soft dough. Knead the dough lightly until it is smooth and free from cracks.
2. Divide the dough into 4 pieces. Shape each one into a ball. Place the rounds close together on a greased and floured baking sheet to form a 'crown'. Brush the tops lightly with milk and sprinkle lightly with granary flour.
3. Bake the bread in a preheated oven for about 25 minutes, or until it is well risen and firm and sounds hollow when tapped underneath.
4. Cool the bread on a wire tray.

From the left: Spinach pancakes; Sage dairy bread

Egg in the Nest

Per serving: 185 Calories, 780 Kilojoules, 20g Protein, 9g Fat,
6g Carbohydrate, 2g Fibre, 325mg Sodium

350g (12oz) potatoes, peeled
225g (8oz) parsnips, peeled and sliced
salt
25g (1oz) soft margarine
5 eggs
freshly ground black pepper
pinch of grated nutmeg
2 tablespoons chopped fresh parsley
75g (3 oz) low-fat hard cheese, grated
sprigs of parsley, to garnish

Preparation time: 15 minutes
Cooking time: 40 minutes
Oven: 190°C, 375°F, Gas Mark 5

1. Cook the potatoes and parsnips in boiling salted water for 15-20 minutes until they are tender. Drain and mash them. Beat in the margarine and 1 of the eggs and season with salt, pepper and nutmeg. Stir in the parsley and 40g (1½oz) of the cheese.
2. Spoon the potato mixture into four 10cm (4 inch) greased individual baking dishes standing on a baking tray, or muffin tins, and shape it to make nests. Make a ridge round the top with a fork. Break 1 egg into each 'nest' and sprinkle the remaining cheese on top.
3. Bake in a preheated oven for 15-20 minutes until the eggs are set. Garnish with the parsley and serve at once.

Vegetable Garden Omelette

Per serving: 310 Calories, 1300 Kilojoules, 22g Protein, 19g Fat,
7g Carbohydrate, 6g Fibre, 370mg Sodium

Serves 2
4 eggs, separated
1 tablespoon water
4 tablespoons cooked peas
4 tablespoons cooked diced carrot
4 tablespoons cooked sweetcorn kernels
2 spring onions, trimmed and chopped
salt
freshly ground black pepper
oil for brushing
40g (1½oz) low-fat hard cheese, grated

Preparation time: 10 minutes
Cooking time: 7-8 minutes

1. In a medium bowl beat the egg yolks and water until they are pale and creamy. In another bowl whisk the egg whites until they are just stiff. Stir the peas, carrot, sweetcorn and onions into the egg yolks and season with salt and pepper. Gently fold the egg whites into the mixture.
2. Brush a 20cm (8inch) omelette pan or frying pan with oil and heat it over a moderate heat.
3. Pour the mixture into the pan and cook the omelette

Sunshine Fruit Kebabs

Per serving: 210 Calories, 880 Kilojoules, 2g Protein, 5g Fat,
25g Carbohydrate, 5g Fibre, 10mg Sodium

2 oranges
2 small grapefruits, peeled and segmented
8 pre-soaked prunes, pitted
4 tablespoons vegetable oil
1 tablespoon red wine vinegar
freshly ground black pepper
2 tablespoons chopped fresh mint
2 tablespoons demerara sugar
8 bay leaves

*Preparation time: 10 minutes, plus marinating
Cooking time: 10 minutes*

1. Peel and segment 1 orange. Cut the other orange in half lengthways. Peel and segment 1 half. Squeeze the juice and grate the rind from the other half.
2. Thread the orange and grapefruit segments and the prunes on to 4 skewers. Place them on a flat dish.
3. In a small bowl mix together the orange juice, orange rind, oil and vinegar, season with pepper and stir in the mint. Pour the dressing over the kebabs and turn them to coat them thoroughly. Set the kebabs aside for at least 1 hour, turning them occasionally if it is convenient.
4. Sprinkle the kebabs with sugar, place them under a preheated moderate grill and cook for 6-7 minutes, turning frequently until the sugar is crisp and the fruit is brown. Thread a bay leaf at both ends of each skewer. Serve hot.

From the left: Egg in the nest; Sunshine fruit kebabs

until the bottom is pale golden brown and the mixture is set. Slide the omelette on to a heatproof serving dish, flipping it to fold in half. Sprinkle the cheese on top and place the dish under a preheated hot grill and cook for 2-3 minutes until it is brown and bubbling. Serve at once.

EVERYDAY EATING

Breakfast in a Glass

Per serving: 270 Calories, 1130 Kilojoules, 12g Protein, 5g Fat, 47g Carbohydrate, 4g Fibre, 180mg Sodium

75g (3oz) porridge oats
300ml (½ pint) skimmed milk
2 large cooking apples, peeled, cored and chopped
grated rind of 1 orange
juice of 2 oranges
300ml (½ pint) buttermilk
2 tablespoons honey
2 eggs
2 tablespoons jumbo oats

Preparation time: 10 minutes, plus soaking and chilling
Cooking time: 10 minutes

1. Soak the porridge oats in the skimmed milk overnight.
2. Put the apple, orange rind, reserving a few strands, and orange juice into a small saucepan, bring to the boil and simmer for 10 minutes or until the apple is tender. Set aside to cool.
3. Place the porridge oats, milk, apple, buttermilk, honey and eggs in a blender and liquidize.
4. Pour the drink into 4 glasses and chill. Sprinkle the jumbo oats and the reserved orange rind on top and serve immediately.

Fruity Vitality Drink

Per serving: 100 Calories, 420 Kilojoules, 8g Protein, 5g Fat, 30g Carbohydrate, 8g Fibre, 100mg Sodium

100g (4oz) dried apricots
150ml (¼ pint) unsweetened orange juice
2.5cm (1 inch) piece of cinnamon stick
2 bananas, peeled and sliced
450ml (¾ pint) plain unsweetened yogurt
2 tablespoons chopped walnuts

Preparation time: 5 minutes, plus soaking and chilling
Cooking time: 20 minutes

1. Soak the apricots in the orange juice for about 3 hours. Tip them into a small saucepan, add the cinnamon, bring to the boil and simmer for 20 minutes or until the apricots are tender. Set aside to cool.
2. Discard the cinnamon and liquidize the apricots with the bananas and yogurt in a blender.
3. Pour the drink into 4 glasses or beakers and chill. Top with the walnuts and serve immediately.

Blackberry and Apple Muesli

Per serving: 340 Calories, 1420 Kilojoules, 10g Protein, 13g Fat, 50g Carbohydrate, 13g Fibre, 35mg Sodium

You can make the muesli mix of the cereals, seeds, nuts and dried fruits in larger quantities and store it in a cool place. Add other fresh fruits according to season. This is an autumn variation. Strawberries and sliced banana, pears and orange segments, and peaches and raspberries are other delicious combinations.

8 tablespoons porridge oats
2 tablespoons jumbo oats
1 tablespoon bran
1 tablespoon sunflower seeds
4 tablespoons mixed chopped nuts
4 tablespoons sultanas
2 dessert apples, cored and thinly sliced
1 tablespoon lemon juice
225g (8oz) blackberries
plain unsweetened yogurt or buttermilk, to serve

Preparation time: 10 minutes

1. Mix together the porridge oats, jumbo oats, bran, sunflower seeds, nuts and sultanas. Toss the sliced apples in the lemon juice.
2. Spoon the muesli mixture into 4 cereal bowls, arrange the apple slices in a ring around the outside and pile the blackberries in the centre. Serve with yogurt or buttermilk for breakfast or a family supper.

Clockwise from top left: Breakfast in a glass; Blackberry and apple muesli; Fruity vitality drink

Fruit Topper

Per serving: 255 Calories, 1065 Kilojoules, 8g Protein, 4g Fat,
50g Carbohydrate, 18g Fibre, 90mg Sodium

*This dish is perfect for a high-fibre breakfast or for
dessert at an informal family meal.*

350g (12 oz) mixed dried fruits (apple rings, apricots,
peaches, pears and prunes)
1 strip thinly pared orange rind
juice of 1 orange
150ml ($\frac{1}{4}$ pint) plain unsweetened yogurt
4 tablespoons muesli
2 tablespoons chopped hazelnuts or almonds

*Preparation time: 10 minutes, plus soaking
Cooking time: 30 minutes*

1. Soak the dried fruit in water to cover for about 3 hours.
2. Measure 300ml ($\frac{1}{2}$ pint) of the soaking water into the
saucepan, add the fruit, the orange rind and orange juice
and bring to the boil. Simmer, uncovered, for 30 minutes or
until the fruit is tender. Set aside to cool.
3. Beat the yogurt and stir in the muesli and the nuts.
4. Serve the fruit with the yogurt mixture swirled on top.

Health Club Sandwiches

Per fruity sandwich: 250 Calories, 1050 Kilojoules, 11g Protein, 3g Fat,
47g Carbohydrate, 8g Fibre, 470mg Sodium
Per vegetable sandwich: 210 Calories, 870 Kilojoules, 10g Protein,
9g Fat, 24g Carbohydrate, 6g Fibre, 380mg Sodium

8 slices black or brown rye bread, or wholewheat bread
175 g (6oz) low-fat soft cheese
75g (3oz) currants
1 teaspoon grated lemon rind
50g (2oz) dried stoned dates, chopped
2 dessert apples, peeled, cored and thinly sliced
1 tablespoon lemon juice
1 kiwi fruit, peeled and thinly sliced into rounds or
2 fresh figs, thinly sliced lengthways
4 mint sprigs, to garnish
150g (5oz) low-fat cottage cheese, sieved
25g (1oz) low-fat hard cheese, grated
2 tablespoons snipped fresh chives
salt
freshly ground black pepper
2 medium carrots, grated
50g (2oz) button mushrooms, thinly sliced
1 tablespoon French dressing
2 hard-boiled eggs, sliced
pinch of paprika

Cabbage Bowl

Per serving: 240 Calories, 1070 Kilojoules, 20g Protein, 11g Fat, 18g Carbohydrate, 8g Fibre, 175mg Sodium

1 small white or green smooth-leaved cabbage
salt
2 chicken pieces
2 tablespoons vegetable oil
1 medium onion, peeled and chopped
1 garlic clove, peeled and crushed
2 large tomatoes, skinned and chopped
1 teaspoon dried oregano
75g (3oz) wholewheat breadcrumbs
75g (3oz) chopped walnuts
freshly ground black pepper
15g ($\frac{1}{2}$oz) soft margarine
1 hard-boiled egg, finely chopped
2 tablespoons chopped fresh parsley

Preparation time: 35 minutes
Cooking time: $1\frac{3}{4}$ hours

1. Remove any discoloured or tough outer leaves from the cabbage and trim it to make a neat, round shape. Blanch the cabbage in a large pan of boiling salted water for 4 minutes, then drain.
2. Skin the chicken pieces, cut the meat from the bones and chop it. (Reserve the bones to make stock for another dish.)
3. Using two large spoons, gently pull the cabbage leaves outwards to make a hollow in the centre. Carefully cut out the centre – a curved grapefruit knife is ideal for this – without cutting through to the base. Finely chop the cabbage centre.
4. Heat the oil in a saucepan and fry the onion and garlic over a moderate heat for 3 minutes, stirring once or twice. Add the chicken and stir frequently for 3 minutes until it is evenly browned. Stir in the chopped cabbage, tomatoes, oregano, 50g (2oz) of the breadcrumbs and 40g (1$\frac{1}{2}$oz) of the walnuts. Season the mixture with salt and pepper and stir for 1 minute.
5. Spoon the filling into the cabbage centre and wrap the whole cabbage tightly in foil. Place the cabbage on a trivet in a large saucepan and half fill the pan with boiling water. Bring the water back to the boil, cover the pan and cook for 1$\frac{1}{2}$ hours, or until the cabbage feels tender when pierced with a fine skewer. Top up the pan with more boiling water from time to time to keep up the level.
6. To make the topping, melt the margarine in a small saucepan, add the remaining breadcrumbs and walnuts and fry over a moderate heat for 3-4 minutes, stirring frequently, until the mixture is dry. Remove from the heat and stir in the chopped egg and parsley.
7. Unwrap the cabbage, place it on a heated serving dish and sprinkle on the topping. Serve it hot, cut into wedges. Boiled new potatoes and tomato sauce go well.

Health club sandwiches

Preparation time: 25 minutes

1. Cut the crusts from the bread.
2. Beat the soft cheese and stir in the currants, lemon rind and dates. Spread 4 of the bread slices with this mixture. Toss the apple slices in the lemon juice to preserve their colour, then arrange them on the sandwich base. Arrange the kiwi fruit or fig slices in a pattern and garnish the open sandwiches with the mint sprigs.
3. Beat the sieved cottage cheese, then beat in the grated cheese and chives. Season with salt and pepper. Spread the remaining 4 bread slices with this mixture. Sprinkle the grated carrot over and press it lightly into the cheese. Toss the mushroom slices in the dressing and arrange them and the hard-boiled egg slices over the carrot topping. Sprinkle a little paprika over the sandwiches.

From the left: Chicken and mushroom pie; Burgundy liver

Chicken and Mushroom Pie

Per serving: 355 Calories, 1475 Kilojoules, 45g Protein, 16g Fat, 5g Carbohydrate, 3g Fibre, 510mg Sodium

Serves 6
1.5kg (3lb) oven-ready chicken with giblets
1 bouquet garni
1 small onion, peeled and quartered
salt
6-8 peppercorns
25g (1oz) soft margarine
2 leeks, trimmed and thinly sliced
100g (4oz) button mushrooms, sliced
1 teaspoon wholewheat flour
100g (4oz) low-fat soft cheese
2 tablespoons chopped fresh parsley
sprigs of parsley, to garnish
<u>Topping:</u>
450g (1lb) potatoes, peeled
225g (8oz) carrots, sliced
25g (1oz) soft margarine
1 egg
pinch of grated nutmeg
freshly ground black pepper

Preparation time: 25 minutes
Cooking time: 1¾ hours
Oven: 190° C, 375° F, Gas Mark 5

1. Wash the chicken and giblets and put them in a large saucepan with the bouquet garni, onion, salt and peppercorns. Cover with water, bring to the boil and skim. Cover the pan and simmer for about 1 hour, or until the chicken is cooked. To test, pierce it through the thickest part of the leg with a fine skewer. The juices should run clear.

2. Lift out the chicken and, when it is cool enough to handle, skin it and cut the meat from the bones. Slice the liver. Place the chicken pieces in a baking dish and set aside. Reserve the chicken stock for soups.

3. Melt the margarine in a small pan and fry the leeks and mushrooms over a moderate heat for 3 minutes, stirring once or twice. Stir in the flour, then the cheese and parsley. Simmer for 3 minutes, then spread the vegetable mixture over the chicken.

4. Cook the potatoes and carrots in boiling salted water for 15-20 minutes, or until they are tender. Drain and mash them and beat in the margarine and egg. Season the mixture with nutmeg, salt and pepper.

5. Spread the vegetable topping evenly over the chicken, then fork it up into peaks.

6. Bake in a preheated oven for 20-25 minutes until the topping is well browned. Garnish with the parsley and serve hot with a green vegetable or a salad.

Burgundy Liver

Per serving: 350 Calories, 1460 Kilojoules, 25g Protein, 20g Fat, 13g Carbohydrate, 2g Fibre, 145mg Sodium

450g (1lb) lamb's liver, thinly sliced
3 tablespoons wholewheat flour
salt
freshly ground black pepper
1 teaspoon dried oregano
1 tablespoon vegetable oil
25g (1oz) soft margarine
1 small onion, peeled and chopped
1 garlic clove, peeled and crushed
1 teaspoon orange rind
juice of 1 orange
120ml (4fl oz) red wine
1 orange sliced, to garnish

Preparation time: 15 minutes
Cooking time: 20 minutes

1. Trim the liver, cutting away any white fibres, and wash and dry it. Mix the flour, salt, pepper and oregano. Cut the liver into thin strips and toss it in the seasoned flour to coat it evenly all over.

2. Heat the oil and margarine in a frying pan and fry the onion and garlic over a moderate heat for about 3 minutes, stirring once or twice. Add the liver and fry for about 3-4 minutes on each side, or until it is cooked just the way you like it. Transfer the liver to a heated serving dish and keep it warm.

3. Add the orange rind and orange juice to the pan, stir quickly and scrape up all the browned flour, then pour on the wine. Season with salt and pepper, bring the sauce to the boil and simmer for 2 minutes.

4. Pour the sauce over the liver and garnish the dish with orange slices. Serve with new potatoes boiled in their jackets and a green vegetable such as tiny French beans.

Tomato Tagliatelle with Vegetable Sauce

Per serving: 310 Calories, **1300** Kilojoules, **12g** Protein, **13g** Fat, **27g** Carbohydrate, **7g** Fibre, **100mg** Sodium

*From the left: Tomato tagliatelle with vegetable sauce;
Cracked wheat risotto*

Delicatessens and other specialist food shops sell fresh yellow (plain egg) pasta, green pasta, which is coloured with spinach, and red, which has had tomato purée added. If necessary substitute dried wholewheat or green pasta, and cook it for about 10 minutes, or according to the directions on the packet.

450g (1lb) fresh red tagliatelle
salt
2 tablespoons vegetable oil
15g ($\frac{1}{2}$oz) soft margarine
2 medium onions, peeled and sliced
2 garlic cloves, peeled and crushed
450g (1lb) courgettes, trimmed and thinly sliced
1 green pepper, cored, seeded and thinly sliced
2 large tomatoes, skinned and chopped
225g (8oz) button mushrooms, sliced
freshly ground black pepper
2 tablespoons chopped fresh parsley
sprigs of oregano, to garnish
<u>Topping:</u>
150g (5oz) low-fat cottage cheese, sieved
25g (1oz) low-fat hard cheese, grated
2 tablespoons chopped fresh parsley
2 tablespoons plain unsweetened yogurt

*Preparation time: 20 minutes
Cooking time: 25 minutes*

1. Cook the tagliatelle in a large pan of lightly salted water for about 5 minutes, or until it is just tender but not soft – 'al dente' as the Italians describe it. Drain the pasta, run hot water through it to prevent it from becoming sticky, and drain it again. Return it to the pan and keep it warm.
2. To make the sauce, heat the oil and margarine in a saucepan and fry the onions over moderate heat for 3 minutes, stirring once or twice. Add the garlic, courgettes and green pepper and fry for 3 minutes. Add the tomatoes and mushrooms, stir well, cover the pan and simmer for 10 minutes, or until the vegetables are just tender. Season with salt and pepper and stir in the parsley.
3. To make the topping, mix together the cottage cheese, grated cheese, parsley and yogurt, and season with pepper.
4. Turn the tagliatelle into a heated serving dish, pour on the sauce and toss with two spoons to distribute it evenly. Spoon the cheese topping into the centre, garnish with sprigs of oregano, and serve at once. A green salad of fresh spinach and endive leaves with a lemon dressing goes well with this colourful pasta dish.

30

Cracked Wheat Risotto

Per serving: 480 Calories, 2010 Kilojoules, 11g Protein, 7g Fat, 29 g Carbohydrate, 13g Fibre, 155mg Sodium

Cracked wheat, also known as burghul or bulgar consists of whole wheat grains which have been boiled until they split, then dried and ground to coarse or fine texture. It is sold in health food shops and in some supermarkets.

25g (1oz) soft margarine
1 large onion, peeled and sliced
1 garlic clove, peeled and chopped
350g (12oz) coarse cracked wheat, washed and drained
100g (4oz) sweetcorn kernels
100g (4oz) shelled peas
4 tablespoons seedless raisins
4 tablespoons sultanas
600ml (1 pint) chicken stock
salt
freshly ground black pepper
4 tablespoons chopped fresh parsley
parsley sprigs, to garnish
1 lemon, quartered, to serve

Preparation time: 15 minutes
Cooking time: 30 minutes

1. Melt the margarine in a frying pan and fry the onion over moderate heat for 3 minutes, stirring once or twice. Add the garlic, cracked wheat, sweetcorn, peas, raisins and sultanas, stir well and pour on the stock. Bring to the boil, cover and simmer over low heat for 15 minutes. Stir well, season with salt and pepper, cover and simmer for a further 5 minutes, or until the cracked wheat is tender and the stock has been absorbed.
2. Stir in the parsley. Turn the risotto on to a heated serving dish and garnish with the parsley sprigs and lemon wedges. Serve hot. This tasty Middle-Eastern style risotto goes well with a green salad or a tomato salad.

Cod Steaks Riviera

Per serving: 155 Calories, 640 Kilojoules, 22g Protein, 5g Fat,
7g Carbohydrate, 3g Fibre, 375mg Sodium

1 large onion, peeled and sliced into rings
1 garlic clove, peeled and crushed
350g (12oz) tomatoes, skinned and sliced
1 tablespoon tomato purée
1 green pepper, cored, seeded and sliced into rings
2 bay leaves
salt
freshly ground black pepper
4 cod steaks
1 tablespoon lemon juice
50g (2oz) stuffed olives, halved
1 tablespoon chopped fresh parsley
<u>To garnish:</u>
25g (1oz) hazelnuts, sliced,
lemon twists
sprigs of parsley

Preparation time: 15 minutes
Cooking time: 30 minutes

1. Put the onion, garlic, tomatoes, tomato purée, green pepper rings and bay leaves into a frying pan. Season with salt and pepper, stir well, bring to the boil, cover and simmer over low heat for 10 minutes.
2. Place the fish steaks on the vegetables, sprinkle on the lemon juice and cover the pan. Simmer for 12-15 minutes, or until the fish is just cooked.
3. Stir in the halved olives and the parsley and just heat through. Using a fish slice, transfer the fish and vegetable sauce to a heated serving dish. Discard the bay leaves. Sprinkle on the hazelnuts and garnish with the lemon twists and sprigs of parsley.

Hake in Parsley Sauce

Per serving: 100 Calories, 420 Kilojoules, 22g Protein, 1g Fat,
Trace Carbohydrate, 1g Fibre, 100mg Sodium

500g (1¼lb) hake, skinned and cut into 2.5cm (1 inch)
slices
1 teaspoon mild curry powder
50g (2oz) parsley sprigs
150ml ($\frac{1}{4}$ pint) fish stock
1 tablespoon dry sherry
1 teaspoon lemon juice
salt
freshly ground black pepper
sprigs of dill, to garnish
1 lemon, sliced, to serve

From the left: Cod steaks riviera; Hake in parsley sauce

Oaty Fish and Sweetcorn Pie

Per serving: 510 Calories, 2130 Kilojoules, 43g Protein, 23g Fat,
36g Carbohydrate, 6g Fibre, 2050mg Sodium

450g (1lb) smoked haddock
450ml (¾ pint) skimmed milk
2 bay leaves
4-5 parsley stalks
6 peppercorns
2 cloves
2 medium carrots, thinly sliced
100g (4oz) sweetcorn kernels
2 rashers bacon, rinded and cut into small squares
25g (1oz) soft margarine
2 tablespoons wholewheat flour
2 hard-boiled eggs, sliced
salt
freshly ground black pepper
Pastry:
75g (3oz) wholewheat flour
25g (1oz) fine oatmeal
1 teaspoon baking powder
50g (2oz) soft margarine
2 tablespoons plain unsweetened yogurt
milk for brushing

Preparation time: 35 minutes
Cooking time: 55 minutes
Oven: 190°C, 375°F, Gas Mark 5

1. Place the haddock in a frying pan with the milk, bay leaves, parsley stalks, peppercorns and cloves. Bring slowly to the boil, cover, and poach the fish for 10 minutes. Lift out the fish and, when it is cool enough to handle, skin and flake it. Strain and reserve the milk.
2. Cook the carrots and sweetcorn in boiling salted water for about 10 minutes, or until tender, then strain them.
3. Fry the bacon in a non-stick saucepan until the fat runs. Lift out the bacon and wipe the pan with a paper towel.
4. Melt the margarine in the saucepan and stir in the flour. Gradually pour on the reserved milk, stirring constantly. Bring to the boil and simmer for 3 minutes. Stir the flaked fish, carrots, sweetcorn, bacon and egg slices into the sauce and season with salt and pepper. Pour the fish mixture into a baking dish and set aside to cool.
5. To make the pastry, mix the flour, oatmeal, baking powder and salt and rub in the margarine. Stir in the yogurt and mix to form a dough. Roll out the pastry and cover the top of the dish. Trim the edges, roll the trimmings and cut out some decorative shapes. Pierce a hole in the centre to allow the steam to escape. Brush the pastry with milk, arrange the decoration and brush the shapes with milk.
6. Bake in a preheated oven for 25-30 minutes. Serve hot.

Preparation time: 15 minutes
Cooking time: 15 minutes

1. Wash, wipe and dry the hake slices. Sprinkle them with the curry powder.
2. Heat a non-stick frying pan and fry the fish over moderate heat for about 8 minutes, turning each slice once. Remove the fish and keep it warm.
3. Add the parsley, fish stock, sherry and lemon juice and season with salt and pepper. Bring the sauce to the boil and boil for 2 minutes. Liquidize the sauce in a blender. Taste and adjust the seasoning if necessary. Pour the sauce on to a heated serving dish, arrange the fish on top and garnish with sprigs of dill. Serve at once with lemon slices. Plain unsweetened yogurt or Greek yogurt and small potatoes boiled in their jackets are good accompaniments.

Malay Fish Curry

Per serving: 320 Calories, 1330 Kilojoules, 26g Protein, 17g Fat, 15g Carbohydrate, 6g Fibre, 175mg Sodium

3 tablespoons vegetable oil
1 medium onion, peeled and chopped
2 teaspoons curry powder
2 teaspoons wholewheat flour
1 teaspoon ground ginger
2 tablespoons lemon juice
150ml ($\frac{1}{4}$ pint) unsweetened orange juice
300ml ($\frac{1}{2}$ pint) water
4 cod steaks, skinned and boned
2 medium carrots, sliced into thin matchstick strips
1 leek, sliced into thin matchstick strips
1 tender celery stick, sliced into thin matchstick strips
salt
freshly ground black pepper
<u>Side dishes:</u>
225g (8oz) firm tomatoes, thinly sliced
1 small onion, peeled and thinly sliced into rings
4 tablespoons vinaigrette dressing
$\frac{1}{4}$ teaspoon ground ginger
1 tablespoon snipped fresh chives
225g (8oz) small French beans, cooked
1 small tomato, skinned, seeded and finely chopped
large pinch of cayenne pepper

Preparation time: 30 minutes
Cooking time: 25 minutes

1. Heat the oil in a frying pan and fry the onion over moderate heat for 3 minutes, stirring once or twice. Stir in the curry powder, flour and ginger and cook for 1 minute. Stir in the lemon juice, orange juice and water and bring to the boil.
2. Add the cod steaks, carrot, leek and celery strips and season with salt and pepper. Bring the sauce to the boil, cover and simmer for 12-15 minutes until the fish and vegetables are tender. Taste the sauce and adjust the seasoning if necessary.
3. Arrange the tomato and onion rings on a small serving dish. Mix together 2 tablespoons of the dressing with the ground ginger and chives and pour it over the vegetables.
4. Arrange the beans on a small serving dish. Mix the chopped tomato and cayenne pepper into the remaining dressing and pour over the beans. Serve the fish curry with brown rice and the tomato and bean side dishes.

Haddock and Cider Casserole

Per serving: 360 Calories, 1500 Kilojoules, 41g Protein, 5g Fat, 36g Carbohydrate, 5g Fibre, 230mg Sodium

1 large onion, peeled and sliced
2 stalks tender celery, thinly sliced
1 garlic clove, peeled and chopped
225g (8oz) tomatoes, skinned and sliced
$\frac{1}{2}$ bunch watercress sprigs, chopped
3 medium potatoes, peeled and finely diced
300ml ($\frac{1}{2}$ pint) medium cider
2 tablespoons orange juice
strip of thinly pared orange rind
salt
freshly ground black pepper
750g (1$\frac{1}{2}$lb) fresh haddock or cod fillet, skinned and cut
into 4cm (1$\frac{1}{2}$ inch) slices
watercress sprigs, to garnish
plain unsweetened yogurt, to serve
<u>Topping:</u>
5 tablespoons jumbo oats
40g (1$\frac{1}{2}$oz) low-fat hard cheese, grated

Preparation time: 15 minutes
Cooking time: 40 minutes

1. Put the onion, celery, garlic and tomatoes into a flame-proof casserole and cook over low heat for 10 minutes, stirring once or twice. Add the chopped watercress, potatoes, cider, orange juice and orange rind. Bring to the boil, cover and simmer for 10 minutes. Season with salt and pepper, add the fish, cover and simmer for 10-12 minutes, or until it is just cooked. Discard the orange rind. Taste the sauce and adjust the seasoning if necessary.
2. Mix together the oats and cheese. Scatter the topping over the dish and cook under a preheated hot grill for 3 minutes, or until the topping is toasty-brown. Garnish with the watercress sprigs and serve hot with chilled yogurt.

From the top: Malay fish curry; Haddock and cider casserole

From the left: Beef and fruit rollers; Stir-fry beef in red sauce

Beef and Fruit Rollers

Per serving: 480 Calories, 2000 Kilojoules, 27g Protein, 27g Fat, 33g Carbohydrate, 3g Fibre, 120mg Sodium

500g (1¼lb) topside of beef, cut into 4 thin slices
75g (3oz) cooked brown rice
1 medium cooking apple, peeled, cored and finely chopped
50g (2oz) seedless raisins, chopped
½ teaspoon grated orange rind
2 tablespoons orange juice
salt
freshly ground black pepper
pinch of grated nutmeg
2 tablespoons fresh mint
2 tablespoons vegetable oil
25g (1oz) soft margarine
1 medium onion, peeled and chopped
1 tablespoon wholewheat flour
150ml (¼ pint) beef stock
150ml (¼ pint) red grape juice
To garnish:
sprigs of mint
orange slices

Preparation time: 40 minutes
Cooking time: 1½ hours

1. Beat the meat slices with a meat bat or wooden rolling pin to flatten and tenderize them. Cut each slice in half.
2. Mix together the rice, apple, raisins, orange rind, orange juice, salt, pepper, nutmeg and 1 tablespoon of the mint.
3. Place the meat slices flat on a board, divide the fruit filling between them and roll them up. Fasten the rolls with twine.
4. Heat the oil and margarine in a flameproof casserole and fry the onion and the beef rolls over moderate heat for 4-5 minutes, turning the beef frequently to brown it evenly on all sides. Lift out the beef rolls, stir in the flour and pour on the stock and grape juice, Season with salt and pepper and bring to the boil, stirring all the time.
5. Return the beef rolls to the dish, cover and simmer for 1¼ hours, turning them occasionally. Taste the sauce, adjust the seasoning if necessary and stir in the remaining mint.
F Serve these tasty fruit-filled rolls hot with brown rice or noodles, garnished with mint sprigs and orange slices.
F Cool, then pack into a rigid container and freeze for up to 3 months. Thaw overnight in the refrigerator; then reheat in a flameproof casserole on the hob, basting occasionally.
M Or turn into a suitable container and microwave, covered, on Defrost for 15-20 minutes separating the rolls when possible. Stand for 10 minutes, then cook on Full (100%) for 10-14 minutes or until hot, stirring once or twice.

Stir-Fry Beef in Red Sauce

Per serving: 410 Calories, 1720 Kilojoules, 26g Protein, 30g Fat, 7g Carbohydrate, 2g Fibre, 75mg Sodium

500g (1¼lb) topside of beef, cut into matchstick strips
2 tablespoons wholewheat flour
salt
freshly ground black pepper
1 teaspoon dried oregano
4 tablespoons vegetable oil
100g (4oz) button mushrooms, sliced
1 medium onion, peeled and sliced
1 garlic clove, peeled and finely chopped
100ml (3½fl oz) beef stock
150ml (¼ pint) red wine
1 teaspoon soy sauce
2-3 drops of hot pepper sauce
steamed broccoli spears, to serve
To garnish:
spring onion curls, (see below)
sprigs of parsley

Preparation time: 20 minutes
Cooking time: 30 minutes

1. Toss the beef in the flour seasoned with salt, pepper and oregano. Lift out the meat and shake off the excess flour.
2. Heat the oil in a heavy-based frying pan or a wok and stir-fry the mushrooms over a moderately high heat for 1 minute. Lift them out onto a plate with a draining spoon. Stir-fry the onion and garlic for 2 minutes. Lift them out onto the plate with a draining spoon.
3. Add the beef to the pan and stir-fry for 4-5 minutes. Pour on the stock, wine, soy and red pepper sauces, return the mushrooms and onions to the pan and bring to the boil. Reduce the heat, cover the pan and simmer for 15-20 minutes, or until the meat is tender. Taste the sauce and adjust the seasoning if necessary.
4. Transfer the meat to a heated serving dish and arrange the broccoli spears in a ring around the outside. Garnish with the spring onion curls and parsley sprigs and serve with noodles or brown rice.

Spring Onion Curls

Remove the roots and trim the spring onions to about 7.5cm (3 inches). Using a sharp knife, make lengthways splits through the stalks to within about 4cm (1½ inches) of the base. Place in a bowl of ice-cold water for about 1 hour and the tops will frill out.

Lamb and Lentil Hotpot

Per serving: 410 Calories, 1730 Kilojoules, 42g Protein, 9g Fat, 44g Carbohydrate, 9g Fibre, 95mg Sodium

Serves 6
275g (10oz) brown continental lentils, soaked for 1-2 hours and drained
1 bay leaf
1kg (2¼lb) lean lamb, trimmed of excess fat and thickly sliced
oil for brushing (optional)
1 large onion, peeled and sliced
4 spring onions, trimmed and sliced
2 garlic cloves, peeled and chopped
350g (12oz) tomatoes, skinned and sliced
150ml (¼ pint) chicken stock
salt
freshly ground black pepper
pinch of ground coriander
3 tablespoons chopped fresh parsley
450g (1lb) potatoes, peeled and thinly sliced

Preparation time: 20 minutes
Cooking time: 2 hours
Oven: 180°C, 350°F, Gas Mark 4

1. Put the lentils into a saucepan, cover with water, add the bay leaf, bring to the boil and simmer for 15 minutes. Drain the lentils in a colander.
2. Dry-fry the meat slices in a non-stick flameproof casserole, or in an oiled casserole, for 3 minutes on each side until they are evenly brown.
3. Lift out the meat with a draining spoon and discard any excess fat. Fry the onions and garlic over moderate heat for 3 minutes, stirring once or twice. Add the lentils, tomatoes and stock and bring to the boil. Season with salt, pepper and coriander and stir in 2 tablespoons of the parsley. Place the potato slices on top and cover the casserole.
4. Cook in a preheated oven for 1¼ hours. Remove the lid and continue cooking for 30 minutes to brown the potatoes. F Sprinkle with the remaining parsley and serve hot with a green vegetable.
F Leave to cool, then skim any fat from the top, cover and freeze for up to 3 months. Thaw overnight in the refrigerator. Cover with foil and heat in a preheated oven for about 45 minutes.

Norfolk Chicken Drumsticks

Per serving: 190 Calories, 790 Kilojoules, 18g Protein, 8g Fat, 14g Carbohydrate, 5g Fibre, 150mg Sodium

8 small chicken drumsticks, skinned
3 tablespoons red wine vinegar
1 tablespoon dark muscovado sugar
1 tablespoon Worcestershire sauce
1 tablespoon tomato purée
½ teaspoon paprika
salt
freshly ground black pepper
½ small lettuce, shredded, to serve
1 small onion, peeled and grated, to serve
2 tomatoes, quartered, to garnish
Sauce:
1 tablespoon vegetable oil
1 small onion, peeled and finely chopped
1 tablespoon red wine vinegar
2 medium carrots, grated
350g (12oz) tomatoes, skinned and chopped
50g (2 oz) seedless raisins
2 tablespoons Dijon mustard

Preparation time: 30 minutes
Cooking time: 35 minutes

1. Make slashes in the chicken flesh so that the flavours can penetrate.
2. In a small saucepan mix together the vinegar, sugar, Worcestershire sauce, tomato purée and paprika and season with salt and pepper. Stir over low heat until the sugar has dissolved, bring to the boil and simmer for 10 minutes. Brush the chicken with the mixture, brushing it well into the flesh.
3. Cook the drumsticks under a preheated medium grill for 25 minutes, turning them frequently and brushing them with any remaining barbecue mixture.
4. Meanwhile, make the sauce. Heat the oil in a small saucepan and fry the onion over moderate heat for 3 minutes, stirring once or twice. Add the vinegar, carrots, tomatoes, raisins and mustard and season with salt and pepper. Bring to the boil and simmer over low heat for 10 minutes. Serve the chicken drumsticks on a bed of shredded lettuce and grated onion, garnished with the tomatoes. Serve the sauce separately.

From the top: Norfolk chicken drumsticks;
Country-style roast lamb

Country-Style Roast Lamb

Per serving: 310 Calories, 1290 Kilojoules, 32g Protein, 12g Fat, 22g Carbohydrate, 9g Fibre, 95mg Sodium

Serves 6

225g (8oz) butter beans, soaked overnight and drained
1.5kg (3lb) shoulder of lamb, trimmed of excess fat
2 garlic cloves, peeled and thinly sliced
2 small sprigs of rosemary, plus some for garnish
225g (8oz) small onions or shallots, peeled
salt
freshly ground black pepper
225g (8oz) tomatoes, skinned and sliced
2 tablespoons chopped fresh parsley
150ml ($\frac{1}{4}$ pint) water

Preparation time: 25 minutes
Cooking time: 1$\frac{3}{4}$ hours
Oven: 190°C, 375°F, Gas Mark 5

1. Cook the butter beans in boiling unsalted water for 1 hour. Drain them.
2. Make slits in the lamb and press in slivers of garlic and small sprigs of rosemary. Place the lamb on a rack in a roasting pan and cook it in a preheated oven for 30 minutes.
3. Lift out the meat, discard the fat and return the meat, without the rack, to the pan. Place the onions around the meat.
4. Season the beans with salt and pepper and stir in the tomatoes and parsley. Spoon the beans around the meat and pour on the water.
5. Return the meat to the oven, cover with foil and cook for a further 45 minutes, or until the meat and the beans are tender. Transfer the meat to a heated serving dish, stir the bean, onion and tomato mixture and adjust the seasoning if necessary. Spoon the vegetables around the meat and garnish with the remaining rosemary. Serve with jacket potatoes cooked in the oven at the same time.

SPECIAL OCCASIONS

Killarney Beef with Potato Thins

Per serving of beef: 415 Calories, 1740 Kilojoules, 49g Protein, 16g Fat, 16g Carbohydrate, 4g Fibre, 215mg Sodium
Per serving of potato: 140 Calories, 590 Kilojoules, 5g Protein, 4g Fat, 25g Carbohydrate, 3g Fibre, 80mg Sodium

3 tablespoons wholewheat flour
freshly ground black pepper
pinch of grated nutmeg
pinch of ground allspice
750g ($\frac{1}{2}$lb) rump steak, trimmed of excess fat
2 tablespoons vegetable oil
1 medium onion, peeled and sliced
2 garlic cloves, peeled and crushed
1 medium carrot, sliced into matchstick strips
1 small turnip, peeled and sliced into matchstick strips
grated rind and juice of 1 orange
300ml ($\frac{1}{2}$ pint) Guinness
salt
To garnish:
2 tablespoons chopped fresh parsley
sprigs of parsley
Potato casserole:
450g (1lb) potatoes, peeled, thinly sliced, washed and dried
1 large onion, peeled and thinly sliced
300ml ($\frac{1}{2}$ pint) skimmed milk
15g ($\frac{1}{2}$oz) soft margarine.

Preparation time: 30 minutes
Cooking time: 1$\frac{3}{4}$ hours
Oven: 180°C, 350°F, Gas Mark 4

1. Mix together the flour, pepper, nutmeg and allspice and rub the mixture into the meat to coat it on both sides.
2. Heat the oil in a flameproof casserole and fry the meat over a moderate heat for 3 minutes on each side to seal and brown it. Lift out the meat and stir-fry the onion, garlic, carrot and turnip in the casserole for 1 minute. Add the orange rind, orange juice and Guinness, season with salt and pepper and bring to the boil. Return the meat to the casserole and spoon the sauce over it and cook, covered, on the lowest shelf of a preheated oven for 1$\frac{1}{2}$ hours.
3. Meanwhile layer some potato slices in a greased baking dish. Cover with a little of the onion and season with salt,

pepper and nutmeg. Make more layers, finishing with potatoes. Pour on the milk and scatter small pieces of the margarine on top. Cover the dish with a lid or foil.
4. Cook on the top shelf of a preheated oven for 1 hour. Remove the cover and continue cooking for 30 minutes.
5. Sprinkle the beef with the chopped parsley, garnish with the sprigs and serve with the potato casserole.

Lamb with Apple Rings

Per serving: 260 Calories, 1090 Kilojoules, 29g Protein, 13g Fat, 9g Carbohydrate, 2g Fibre, 75mg Sodium

8 small noisettes of lamb, trimmed of excess fat
2 tablespoons wholewheat flour
freshly ground black pepper
$\frac{1}{2}$ teaspoon dried oregano
vegetable oil for brushing (optional)
150ml ($\frac{1}{4}$ pint) chicken stock
1 teaspoon grated orange rind
2 tablespoons orange juice
8 dried apple rings, soaked for 1-2 hours and drained
salt
sprigs of oregano, to garnish

Preparation time: 10 minutes
Cooking time: 25 minutes

1. Dry the lamb and toss it in the flour seasoned with pepper and oregano. Place the noisettes in a non-stick frying pan over a moderate heat (or brush a pan lightly with oil) and fry for about 3 minutes on each side until they are evenly browned. Reduce the heat and cook them for about 10 minutes, turning them once, until they are cooked the way you like them. Transfer the noisettes to a heated serving dish and keep them warm. Wipe the frying pan with a paper towel to remove any traces of fat.
2. Add the stock, orange rind, orange juice and apple rings to the pan, season with salt and pepper and bring to the boil. Lower the heat and simmer for 5 minutes or until the apple rings are just tender.
3. Pour the sauce over the lamb, arrange the apple rings and garnish with the oregano. Serve with tiny new carrots and fresh garden peas, calabrese or broccoli spears.

From the top: Lamb with apple rings; Killarney beef with potato thins

Grilled Duck Breasts with Fiery Apple Sauce

Per serving: 493 Calories, 2070 Kilojoules, 45g Protein, 29g Fat, 15g Carbohydrate, 2g Fibre, 210mg Sodium

If you cannot obtain fresh or bottled horseradish, use about 1 tablespoon creamed horseradish.

4 boneless duck breasts, about 225g (8oz) each, skinned
2 tablespoons vegetable oil
4 tablespoons apple juice
2 tablespoons clear honey
1 tablespoon finely chopped peeled fresh root ginger
1 garlic clove, peeled and crushed
salt
freshly ground black pepper
celery curls (below) to garnish
Sauce:
15g (½oz) soft margarine
2 medium cooking apples, peeled, cored and sliced
1 shallot or small onion, peeled and chopped
2 tablespoons lemon juice
2 teaspoons peeled fresh root ginger
1 teaspoon grated fresh horseradish
(or bottled horseradish, rinsed and drained)
fresh coriander sprig, to garnish

*Preparation time: 20 minutes, plus marinating
Cooking time: 25 minutes*

1. Using a sharp knife, make criss-cross slits in the duck flesh so that the marinade flavours can penetrate. Place the duck portions in a shallow dish.
2. Mix together the oil, apple juice, honey, ginger and garlic and season the marinade with salt and pepper. Brush the mixture over the duck pieces on all sides, brushing it well into the flesh. Cover and set aside for 1-2 hours.
3. Place the duck under a preheated moderate grill and cook for 15-20 minutes, turning the pieces over frequently so they cook evenly on all sides.
4. To make the sauce, put the margarine, apple, shallot, lemon juice, ginger and horseradish into a small saucepan, season with salt and pepper and simmer for 8-10 minutes, shaking the pan frequently, until the apples are tender, then mash them into a purée. Serve the duck garnished with celery curls and a green vegetable such as stir-fried mange-touts, garnished with a fresh coriander sprig. Serve the apple sauce separately, garnished with a fresh coriander sprig.

From the left: Grilled duck breasts with fiery apple sauce; Greek-style lamb

Celery Curls

Cut celery sticks into even lengths, about 10cm (4 inches) long. With a sharp knife, make slits from one end to the centre. Place the celery in ice-cold water for about 1 hour. The slits will frill out, like a tassel. Drain and dry them.

1. Pat the meat dry. Cut slits and insert the slices of garlic.
2. Mix together the oil, wine, lemon juice and herb and season with salt and pepper.
3. Cut six 20cm (8inch) squares of foil and brush the centre of each lightly with oil. Divide the lamb slices between them, draw up the sides slightly and pour on the dressing. Fold over the foil and seal the joins tightly so that the parcels do not leak. Set aside for at least 2 hours to marinate. F
4. Place the foil parcels on a baking sheet and cook in a preheated oven for 2 hours. Unwrap the parcels and place the lamb on a serving dish. Garnish with the sprigs of parsley and, in the Greek way, pass round wedges of lemon to squeeze over the meat. Serve with potatoes cooked in the oven at the same time, and a green vegetable such as spinach or a green salad.

F Freeze the uncooked lamb parcels with the marinade, for up to 3 months. You can cook them from frozen. Increase the oven temperature to 180°C, 350°F, Gas Mark 4 for the first 30 minutes of the cooking time.

New England Boiled Beef

Per serving: 550 Calories, 2200 Kilojoules, 85g Protein, 13g Fat, 25g Carbohydrate, 6g Fibre, 2640mg Sodium

Serves 6
1.75kg (4lb) salt beef, trimmed of excess fat
1 bouquet garni
450g (1lb) potatoes, peeled and thickly sliced
225g (8oz) carrots, thickly sliced
225g (8oz) swede, peeled and cubed
225g (8oz) turnip, peeled and cubed
12 small onions or shallots, peeled
$\frac{1}{2}$ small, firm white cabbage, thickly sliced
1 small head celery, thickly sliced
freshly ground black pepper
3 tablespoons chopped fresh parsley, to garnish

Preparation time: 25 minutes
Cooking time: 3$\frac{1}{2}$ hours

1. Put the beef in a large flameproof casserole or saucepan. Cover the meat with cold water, add the bouquet garni and bring to the boil. Skim any foam that rises to the surface. Cover and simmer for 3 hours, topping up with more boiling water to keep the meat covered.
2. Add the potato, carrot, swede and turnip. Bring the stock back to the boil, cover and simmer for 10 minutes.
3. Add the onions or shallots, cabbage and celery, season with pepper, bring to the boil, cover and simmer for 10 minutes, or until all the vegetables are just tender.
4. Slice the meat thickly and arrange it on a heated serving dish surrounded by the drained vegetables, sprinkled with parsley. Skim the fat from the surface and serve a little of the well-flavoured stock separately. Keep the rest for soup.

Greek-Style Lamb

Per serving: 480 Calories, 1990 Kilojoules, 30g Protein, 39g Fat, Trace Carbohydrate, Trace Fibre, 90mg Sodium

Serves 6
1kg (2$\frac{1}{4}$lb) boned leg of lamb, cut into 2.5cm (1 inch) slices
4 garlic cloves, peeled and thinly sliced
3 tablespoons vegetable oil, plus extra for brushing
5 tablespoons red wine
1 tablespoon lemon juice
2 tablespoons chopped fresh marjoram, or 1 teaspoon dried oregano
salt
freshly ground black pepper
sprigs of parsley, to garnish
1 lemon, sliced into wedges, to serve

Preparation time: 1 hour, plus marinating
Cooking time: 2 hours
Oven: 160°C, 325°F, Gas Mark 3

Clay-Baked Chicken with Pecan Stuffing

Per serving: 440 Calories, 1840 Kilojoules, 49g Protein, 26g Fat, 8g Carbohydrate, 3g Fibre, 270mg Sodium

If you do not have a chicken brick, cook the chicken on a rack in a roasting pan in a preheated oven at 190° C, 375° F, Gas Mark 5 for 1¼ hours or until the chicken is cooked. Test it by piercing through the thickest part of the thigh with a fine skewer. The juices should run clear.

1.5kg (3lb) oven-ready chicken, washed and dried
2 tablespoons lemon juice
freshly ground black pepper
1 tablespoon vegetable oil
Stuffing:
25g (1oz) soft margarine
1 small onion, peeled and chopped
50g (2oz) mushrooms, chopped
50g (2oz) wholewheat breadcrumbs
50g (2oz) chopped pecan nuts
1 teaspoon orange rind
3 tablespoons orange juice
2 tablespoons chopped fresh parsley
1 teaspoon fresh thyme, or ½ teaspoon dried thyme
pinch of grated nutmeg
pinch of ground mace
salt

To garnish:
carrot and olive flowers (right)
bay leaves
sprigs of thyme
sprigs of parsley

Preparation time: 25 minutes, plus soaking
Cooking time: 1½ hours
Oven (not preheated): 240° C, 475° F, Gas Mark 9

1. Soak the chicken brick in water for 20 minutes. To make the stuffing, melt the margarine in a small saucepan and fry the onion over moderate heat for 2 minutes. Stir in the mushrooms and cook for 2 minutes. Stir in the breadcrumbs and remove the pan from the heat. Stir in the nuts, orange rind and juice, herbs and spices. Season with salt and pepper.
2. Pack the filling into the chicken and close the vents with skewers or sew with a poultry needle and strong twine. Season the outside of the chicken with lemon juice and pepper and rub it lightly with oil.
3. Remove the brick from the water. Place a piece of greaseproof paper in the bottom, put the chicken on it and put on the lid.
4. Put the chicken brick in an unheated oven and set it to the temperature indicated. Cook for 1½ hours.
5. Remove the chicken from the brick. Pour off the juices from the brick, skim the fat and use it to make gravy if wished. Place on a serving dish and garnish the chicken with the olive and carrot flowers and the fresh herbs. Serve with boiled potatoes, tossed in a little lemon rind and lemon juice, and a green vegetable, such as broccoli spears garnished with chopped pecans.

From the left: Clay-baked chicken with pecan stuffing;
Poussins with spicy herb sauce

Poussins with Spicy Herb Sauce

Per serving: 470 Calories, 1960 Kilojoules, 57g Protein, 19g Fat, 19g Carbohydrate, 1g Fibre, 260mg Sodium

4 oven-ready poussins, about 450g (1lb) each
with giblets, washed and dried
1 tablespoon wholewheat flour
1 tablespoon Dijon mustard
150ml ($\frac{1}{4}$ pint) chicken stock
2 tablespoons chopped fresh dill
100ml (3$\frac{1}{2}$oz) plain unsweetened yogurt
1 teaspoon cornflour
sprigs of fresh dill, to garnish
<u>Stuffing:</u>
25g (1oz) soft margarine
1 small onion, peeled and chopped
4 poussin livers, washed, dried and chopped
8 tablespoons cooked brown rice
2 tablespoons chopped fresh dill
salt
freshly ground black pepper
pinch of grated nutmeg
1 egg

Preparation time: 20 minutes
Cooking time: about 1 hour
Oven: 180°C, 350°F, Gas Mark 4

1. To make the stuffing, melt the margarine in a small saucepan and fry the onion over a moderate heat for 2 minutes. Stir in the chopped livers and fry for 2 minutes. Stir in the rice. Remove the pan from the heat, stir in the herbs and season with salt, pepper and nutmeg. Beat in the egg.
2. Pack the stuffing into the cavity in the birds. Close the vents with skewers, or sew with a poultry needle and twine. Place the birds on a rack in a roasting pan.
3. Cook the poussins in a preheated oven for 45–50 minutes, turning them once and basting them frequently with the pan juices.
4. Transfer the poussins to a heated serving dish. Remove the rack from the pan and skim the fat. Stir in the flour and mustard and cook for 1 minute. Pour on the stock and, stirring constantly, bring to the boil. Stir in the dill. Beat the yogurt and stir in the cornflour – this will prevent the yogurt from separating. Add it to the sauce in the pan, season with salt, pepper and nutmeg and simmer for about 2 minutes. Pour the sauce over the poussins, garnish with the sprigs of dill and serve at once. Serve with spring vegetables such as tiny broad beans cooked in their shells or mange-touts and new potatoes.

Carrot and Olive Flowers

Carrots and olives (both black and green) make stunning 'flowers', either together or separately. For carrot flowers, choose cylindrically-shaped carrots if possible. Cook them as usual, then cut them into thin slices. Using small aspic cutters, cut each slice into a decorative shape. Assemble them as a bunch of flowers, using chive leaves as the stalks. To make olive flowers, using a small sharp knife, cut 4 or 5 very thin slices from each olive, working around the stone. Arrange these petal shapes to resemble a flower or combine them with the carrot flowers.

Saddle of Rabbit with Flageolets

Per serving: 420 Calories, 1710 Kilojoules, 40g Protein, 17g Fat, 21g Carbohydrate, 10g Fibre, 170mg Sodium

Serves 6
2 saddles of rabbit, about 1.5kg (3½lb) total weight
225g (8oz) dried flageolet beans, soaked overnight and drained
25g (1oz) soft margarine
1 large onion, peeled and sliced
2 celery sticks, thinly sliced
4 garlic cloves, peeled and chopped
450ml (¾ pint) chicken stock
salt
freshly ground black pepper
1 orange, thinly sliced, to garnish
Marinade:
3 tablespoons vegetable oil
4 juniper berries, crushed
6 peppercorns, crushed
1 medium onion, peeled and chopped
few stalks of parsley
2 sprigs fresh thyme
150ml (¼ pint) dry white wine

Preparation time: 30 minutes, plus marinating and soaking
Cooking time: 2¼ hours
Oven: 180°C, 350°F, Gas Mark 4

1. Put all the marinade ingredients into a small saucepan, bring to the boil, then set aside to cool. Place the rabbit in a strong polythene bag or a shallow dish, pour on the marinade, turn the meat over and over and seal the bag or cover the dish. Set aside to marinate for at least 3 hours, turning the meat once or twice if it is convenient.
2. Cook the beans in boiling unsalted water for 15 minutes, then drain them.
3. Lift the rabbit from the marinade and wrap each saddle closely in greased foil. Strain and reserve the marinade. Place the rabbit in a roasting pan and cook it in a preheated oven for 30 minutes.
4. Melt the margarine in a flameproof casserole and fry the onion, celery and garlic over moderate heat for 3 minutes, stirring once or twice. Add the beans, chicken stock and reserved marinade. Bring to the boil, cover the casserole dish and cook in the preheated oven for 1¾ hours, until the beans are tender and the sauce is creamy. Season them with salt and pepper.
5. Unwrap the rabbit and place the 2 saddles on a heated serving dish. Spoon the beans around it and garnish with the orange slices.

Casserole of Pheasant with Dried Apricots

Per serving: 445 Calories, 1860 Kilojoules, 50g Protein, 17g Fat, 23g Carbohydrate, 10g Fibre, 210mg Sodium

Serves 6
25g (1oz) soft margarine
1 brace of oven-ready pheasants, washed and dried
225g (8oz) small onions or shallots, peeled
1 tablespoon wholewheat flour
450ml (¾ pint) chicken stock
1 tablespoon clear honey
2 teaspoons orange rind
3 tablespoons orange juice
1 bay leaf
225g (8oz) dried whole apricots, soaked for 2-3 hours and drained
salt
freshly ground black pepper
2 tablespoons chopped fresh parsley, to garnish (optional)

Preparation time: 30 minutes, plus soaking
Cooking time: 2 hours
Oven: 180°C, 350°F, Gas Mark 4

1. Melt the margarine in a flameproof casserole and fry the pheasants over moderate heat for 10 minutes, turning the birds frequently to brown them evenly. Lift out the pheasants and keep them warm. Fry the onions in the casserole for 2-3 minutes, stirring them once or twice, then stir in the flour. Pour on the chicken stock, stirring all the time, then add the honey, orange rind, orange juice, bay leaf and apricots, and season with salt and pepper. Bring the sauce to the boil, stirring occasionally.
2. Return the pheasants and cover the casserole. Cook in a preheated oven for 1½ hours, or until the birds are tender.
3. Lift out the pheasants and cut them into joints – a pair of poultry shears is a help. Lift out the onions and apricots with a draining spoon and arrange them around the meat. Discard the bay leaf.
4. Boil the sauce over moderate heat for 5-10 minutes to reduce and thicken it. Taste it and adjust the seasoning if necessary. Pour the sauce over the pheasants and garnish with the parsley, if wished. Serve this rich and tasty game dish with steamed cauliflower and small potatoes, and a crisp green salad.

Casserole of pheasant with dried apricots

From the left: Rack of lamb on spiced rice; Balkan-style beef

Rack of Lamb on Spiced Rice

Per serving: 670 Calories, 2810 Kilojoules, 47g Protein, 30g Fat, 60g Carbohydrate, 5g Fibre, 230mg Sodium

Serves 6

2 racks of lamb, each with 6-7 cutlets, chined, skinned and trimmed of excess fat
175g (6oz) brown rice
50g (2oz) seedless raisins
50g (2oz) blanched almond slivers
3 tablespoons clear honey
1 tablespoon mustard powder
2 tablespoons grated orange rind
8 tablespoons wholewheat breadcrumbs
sprigs of parsley, to garnish

Marinade:
3 tablespoons vegetable oil
4 tablespoons dry sherry
2 tablespoons soy sauce
1 tablespoon red wine vinegar
1 tablespoon honey
1 teaspoon ground cinnamon
2 teaspoons grated orange rind
juice of 1 orange
1 medium onion, peeled and chopped

48

to the oven and cook for another 15–20 minutes, until it is cooked the way you like it.

5. Stand the 2 racks of lamb side by side on a heated serving dish, the bones interlocking. Decorate the bone ends with cutlet frills if you have them. Spoon the rice around the lamb and garnish the dish with parsley. Serve with broccoli, French beans or peas.

Balkan-Style Beef

Per serving: 560 Calories, 2340 Kilojoules, 60g Protein, 33g Fat, 8g Carbohydrate, 3g Fibre, 225mg Sodium

750g (1½lb) fillet steak
4 tablespoons vegetable oil
25g (1oz) soft margarine
1 medium onion, peeled and chopped
350g (12oz) small button mushrooms
(or large ones, sliced)
300ml (½ pint) plain unsweetened yogurt
1 tablespoon Dijon mustard
salt
freshly ground black pepper
large pinch of paprika
2 tablespoons chopped fresh parsley, to garnish

Preparation time: 25 minutes
Cooking time: 20 minutes

1. Wipe and dry the meat. Cut it across the grain into 1cm (½ inch) slices. Cut the slices into 5cm (2 inch) strips.
2. Heat 2 tablespoons of the oil and the margarine in a frying pan and fry the onion over moderate heat for 3 minutes, stirring once or twice. Add the mushrooms, stir well and fry for 2-3 minutes, until they are just beginning to soften. Lift out the vegetables with a draining spoon.
3. Heat the remaining oil and fry the steak over moderately high heat for 3-4 minutes, stirring it constantly to brown it evenly.
4. Stir in the mustard and season with salt and pepper. Simmer the sauce for 2 minutes. Stir in the vegetables and yogurt and just heat through. Do not let the yogurt boil or it will curdle.
5. Turn the beef on to a heated serving dish, sprinkle it with the paprika and parsley. Serve at once with wholewheat or green noodles and a green vegetable – spinach and sorrel both go specially well.

Preparation time: 30 minutes, plus marinating
Cooking time: 1 hour
Oven: 200° C, 400° F, Gas Mark 6

1. Put all the marinade ingredients into a small saucepan, bring to the boil, then set aside to cool. Put the lamb into a strong polythene bag or a dish, pour on the marinade, turn the meat to coat it thoroughly, and seal the bag or cover the dish. Set aside for 5-6 hours. Lift out the meat and dry it. Strain and reserve the marinade.
2. Measure the marinade and make it up to 450ml (¾ pint) with water. Put the rice, raisins, almonds and liquid into a saucepan, stir well, then bring to the boil and simmer over low heat for 40-45 minutes, or until the rice is just tender.
3. Make diagonal cuts in the lamb fat, to make diamond patterns. Place the lamb on a rack in a roasting pan and cook in a preheated oven for 20 minutes.
4. Mix together the honey and mustard and brush the paste over the lamb fat. Mix the orange rind and breadcrumbs and press into the honey paste to coat the lamb. Return the lamb

49

Baked Brixham Crab

From the left: Baked Brixham crab;
Grilled red mullet with fennel and dill

Per serving: 280 Calories, 1170 Kilojoules, 34g Protein, 14g Fat,
6g Carbohydrate, Trace Fibre, 720mg Sodium

4 small fresh crabs, dressed
2 tablespoons double cream
pinch of cayenne pepper
1 tablespoon chopped parsley
salt
freshly ground black pepper
1 teaspoon cornflour
300ml ($\frac{1}{2}$ pint) plain unsweetened yogurt
1 teaspoon made mustard
75g (3oz) low-fat hard cheese, grated
2 eggs, beaten
To garnish:
cucumber cones (right)
sprigs of parsley
lemon cones (right)
sprigs of dill

Preparation time: 30 minutes
Cooking time: 30 minutes
Oven: 200°C, 400°F, Gas Mark 6

1. Scoop out the white and the brown crab meat into separate bowls. Mix the brown meat with the cream, cayenne pepper and parsley and season it with a little salt and pepper. Spoon the crab mixture into the 4 shells.
2. Stir the cornflour into the yogurt to stabilize it, to stop it separating when cooked. Stir in the mustard and 25g (1oz) of the cheese, and beat in the eggs. Season with salt and pepper and stir in the white crab meat. Spoon the mixture over the crab shells and sprinkle on the remaining cheese.
3. Stand the crab shells on a baking sheet and cook in a preheated oven for 20-25 minutes until the cheese topping is golden brown and bubbling. Garnish with cucumber cones filled with parsley sprigs and lemon cones filled with dill and serve at once.

Cucumber and Lemon Cones

Take thin slices of cucumber or lemon (remove the pips). Make a cut from the edge to the centre (the radius of the circle). Hold each cut side and twist the slice to form a cone – the cut sides will overlap and the natural moisture will hold them together.

1. Wash and dry the fish and make 3 slashes in each side. Season them inside and out with salt and pepper. Halve 1 lemon and squeeze the juice into the fish cavity. Brush the fish all over with olive oil, place a piece of onion in each one and cover them with fresh dill.

2. Brush the grill rack with oil and place a 'mat' of several fennel stalks on it, if available. Place the fish on the rack and cook them under a preheated medium grill for about 5 minutes on each side or until they are just tender.

3. Put the grapes in a small pan with the orange juice and simmer over moderate heat for 5 minutes or until they are tender. Lift out the grapes with a draining spoon.

4. Serve the fish at once, garnished with the grapes, lemon quarters and sprigs of parsley.

Scampi with Flamed Brandy Sauce

Per serving: 455 Calories, 1900 Kilojoules, 17g Protein, 25g Fat, 40g Carbohydrate, 4g Fibre, 510mg Sodium

25g (1oz) soft margarine
2 medium onions, peeled and chopped
1 garlic clove, peeled and chopped
450g (1lb) raw, shelled scampi, defrosted if frozen
salt
freshly ground black pepper
3 tablespoons brandy
1 teaspoon orange rind
juice of 1 orange
1 teaspoon cornflour
8 tablespoons plain unsweetened yogurt
100g (4oz) button mushrooms, thinly sliced
4 tablespoons chopped fresh parsley
pinch of cayenne pepper

Preparation time: 15 minutes
Cooking time: 15 minutes, plus cooking the rice

1. Heat 15g ($\frac{1}{2}$oz) of the margarine in a frying-pan and fry the onion and garlic over moderate heat for 2 minutes, stirring once or twice. Add the scampi, season with salt and pepper and fry for 3-4 minutes, stirring frequently. Pour on the brandy, shake the pan well and set light to it with a match. Tip the pan – taking great care because of the flames – so that the spirit burns evenly.

2. Add the orange rind and orange juice. Stir the cornflour into the yogurt and stir into the pan. Taste the sauce, adjust the seasoning if necessary, and simmer for 4-5 minutes.

3. Melt the remaining margarine in a small pan and stir-fry the mushrooms for 2 minutes.

4. Stir the mushrooms and the remaining parsley into the scampi and spoon the scampi into the centre of a heated serving dish with a ring of plain boiled rice around it.

Grilled Red Mullet with Fennel and Dill

Per serving: 375 Calories, 1570 Kilojoules, 60g Protein, 11g Fat, 10g Carbohydrate, 1g Fibre, 225mg Sodium

4 red mullet, each about 400g (14oz), cleaned and gutted
salt
freshly ground black pepper
2 lemons
olive oil, for brushing
1 medium onion, peeled and quartered
handful of fresh dill
fennel stalks, if available
175g (6oz) green grapes, seeded
3 tablespoons orange juice
To garnish:
lemon quarters
sprigs of parsley

Preparation time: 25 minutes
Cooking time: 15 minutes

Oriental Steamed Grey Mullet

Per serving: 495 Calories, 2070 Kilojoules, 60g Protein, 23g Fat, 10g Carbohydrate, 1g Fibre, 260mg Sodium

1 grey mullet, about 1.25kg (2½lb), gutted and cleaned
2 tablespoons orange juice
freshly ground black pepper
4 tender celery sticks, thinly sliced
spring onion curls, to garnish (page 37)
Sauce:
2 teaspoons cornflour
4 tablespoons soy sauce
4 tablespoons dry sherry
2 tablespoons clear honey
3 tablespoons vegetable oil
2 tablespoons red wine vinegar
1 teaspoon finely chopped peeled root ginger

Preparation time: 20 minutes
Cooking time: 30 minutes

1. Make the sauce. Put the cornflour into a small bowl, pour on the soy sauce, stirring constantly, to make a smooth paste, then stir in the remaining sauce ingredients.
2. Wash and dry the fish and sprinkle it inside and out with orange juice. Season it with pepper.
3. Place the fish on a shallow heatproof dish, curving it round to fit the container. Scatter the celery and sliced onion over the fish and pour on the sauce.
4. Place the dish in the top part of a steaming pan, or over a pan of fast-boiling water. Cover the dish with a lid or foil and steam for 25 minutes or until the fish is just tender.
5. Serve the fish whole with the sweet and sour sauce, and garnish with spring onion curls. Serve with long-grain brown rice or Chinese noodles.

Baked Orange Trout

Per serving: 380 Calories, 1600 Kilojoules, 18g Protein, 16g Fat, 44g Carbohydrate, 5g Fibre, 250mg Sodium

4 fresh trout, about 275g (10oz) each, gutted and cleaned
8 tablespoons wholewheat breadcrumbs
1 tablespoon grated orange rind
juice of 1 orange
2 tablespoons chopped fresh coriander, or parsley
2 tablespoons pine nuts
4 tablespoons seedless raisins, chopped
salt
freshly ground black pepper
pinch of ground allspice
1 small egg, beaten
oil, for brushing
To garnish:
shredded lettuce
sprigs of watercress
orange slices
Sauce:
3 tablespoons clear honey
1 tablespoon vegetable oil
2 teaspoons grated orange rind
juice of 2 oranges
3 tablespoons water
50g (2oz) seedless raisins

Preparation time: 25 minutes
Cooking time: 30 minutes
Oven: 190°C, 375°F, Gas Mark 5

1. Wash and dry the trout. In a bowl mix together the breadcrumbs, orange rind, orange juice, herb, pine nuts and raisins and season with salt, pepper and allspice. Bind the stuffing with the beaten egg.
2. Spoon the filling into the trout cavities and close the openings with skewers. Brush the trout with oil and season well with pepper.
3. Place the trout in a shallow, oiled baking dish. Cook in a preheated oven for 20-25 minutes, turning the fish once. When the fish are perfectly cooked the skins should be crisp and bubbling.
4. Put all the ingredients for the sauce into a small saucepan, stir over low heat and bring just to the boil.
5. Place the fish on a bed of shredded lettuce, pour the sauce over and garnish with sprigs of watercress and slices of orange. Serve with new potatoes and baked tomatoes.

From the left: Baked orange trout; Harbourside kebabs

Harbourside Kebabs

Per serving: 390 Calories, **1630** Kilojoules, **43**g Protein, **15**g Fat, 21g Carbohydrate, 5g Fibre, 1480mg Sodium

oil, for brushing
450g (1lb) fresh haddock or cod fillet, skinned and cut into 3cm (1¼ inch) slices
2 small heads corn-on-the cob, cut into 2cm (¾ inch) slices
350g (12oz) large raw, peeled prawns
2 courgettes, trimmed and cut into 2.5cm (1 inch) slices
8 bay leaves
Marinade:
3 tablespoons vegetable oil
4 tablespoons lemon juice
2 tablespoons chopped fresh parsley
2 bay leaves, crumbled
1 small onion, peeled and finely chopped
2 teaspoons finely chopped peeled root ginger
salt
freshly ground black pepper

Preparation time: 15 minutes, plus marinating
Cooking time: 10 minutes

1. Mix together all the marinade ingredients.
2. Brush 4 skewers with oil and thread the fish, corn, prawns and courgette slices on to them.
3. Place the kebabs in a shallow dish, pour over the marinade and turn the kebabs to coat them thoroughly. Cover and set aside in a cool place to marinate for 2-3 hours, turning the kebabs once or twice if it is convenient.
4. Cook the kebabs under a preheated hot grill for 6-8 minutes, turning them frequently and brushing them with the remaining marinade and a little extra oil if necessary. Thread a bay leaf on to each end of the skewers and serve at once, garnished with onion rings and parsley sprigs, and a dish of sliced tomatoes with a vinaigrette dressing.

53

From the left: Summer buffet terrine; Pimento chicken

Summer Buffet Terrine

Per small serving: 165 Calories, 690 Kilojoules, 23g Protein, 6g Fat, 3g Carbohydrate, 1g Fibre, 170mg Sodium

Preparation time: 1 hour, plus marinating and chilling
Cooking time: 1 hour
Oven: 190°C, 375°F, Gas Mark 5

Serves 8-10
225g (8oz) salmon fillet
6 tablespoons white wine
3 tablespoons lemon juice
1 small onion, peeled and chopped
salt
freshly ground black pepper
750g (1½lb) haddock fillet, skinned
2 egg whites and 1 egg yolk
1 teaspoon cornflour
300ml (½ pint) plain unsweetened yogurt
¼ teaspoon cayenne pepper
6 tablespoons chopped fresh parsley
50g (2oz) button mushrooms, thinly sliced
<u>To garnish:</u>
1 red pepper, cored, seeded and cut into leaf shapes
5 small bay leaves
chives
1 teaspoon aspic crystals
4 tablespoons chicken stock
1 tablespoon sherry

1. Skin the salmon and cut it into 2cm (¾inch) wide strips. In a bowl mix together 3 tablespoons of the wine, the lemon juice and onion and season with salt and pepper. Place the salmon in this mixture, cover and set aside to marinate for about 30 minutes.
2. Finely mince the haddock, or work it in a food processor until it has the consistency of a coarse paste. Gradually beat in the egg white. Stir the cornflour into the yogurt and beat in the egg yolk and beat this into the fish mixture. Season the mixture with the cayenne, salt and pepper – it should taste quite spicy. Stir in 3 tablespoons of the parsley.
3. Dry the salmon strips with paper towels and toss them in the remaining parsley.
4. Line a 750g (1½lb) loaf tin with foil. Spread one third of the white fish mixture over the base. Cover this with the mushrooms, then cover them with another third of the fish mixture and then the salmon strips (running from end to end of the tin). Finally, cover the salmon with the remaining white fish. Cover the tin with foil.
5. Stand the tin in a roasting pan with cold water reaching half-way up the sides. Cook in a preheated oven for 50

minutes, or until a fine skewer inserted into the terrine comes out clean.

6. Stand the tin on a wire rack to cool. Ⓐ Ⓕ Peel off the foil and place the terrine on a serving dish. Arrange the red pepper shapes, small bay leaves and chives in a pattern on the top. Dissolve the aspic crystals in the chicken stock, stir in the sherry and leave until the mixture becomes syrupy. Pour the glaze over the terrine and brush it to cover the decoration. Chill for about 1 hour.

Ⓐ Make the day before and chill overnight.

Ⓕ The terrine freezes well. Cool it completely, wrap in a strong polythene bag or in more foil, and store for up to 2 months. You can complete the decoration and glaze as the terrine thaws in the refrigerator.

Pimento Chicken

Per serving: 445 Calories, 1860 Kilojoules, 39g Protein, 30g Fat, 4g Carbohydrate, 2g Fibre, 235mg Sodium

Serves 8
1.75kg (4lb) oven-ready chicken
1 medium onion, peeled and quartered
1 carrot, sliced
2 celery sticks, sliced
4 juniper berries, crushed
1 bay leaf
4-6 stalks parsley
salt
6 peppercorns, lightly crushed
1 red pepper, cored, seeded and thinly sliced into rings
4 large tomatoes, thinly sliced (optional)
sprigs of watercress, to garnish
Sauce:
225g (8oz) canned pimentos, drained, rinsed and chopped
1 tablespoon tomato purée
2 tablespoons mango chutney, chopped
200 ml (7fl oz) mayonnaise
freshly ground black pepper

Preparation time: 1 hour
Cooking time: 2¼ hours

1. Put the chicken, onion, carrot, celery, juniper berries, bay leaf, parsley stalks, salt and peppercorns into a saucepan. Cover the chicken with water. Bring to the boil and skim any foam that rises to the surface. Cover the saucepan and simmer for 1½-2 hours, or until the chicken is tender.

2. Leave the chicken to cool in the stock – this will prevent it from drying out. Lift out the chicken, drain and dry it. (Reserve the stock). Skin the chicken and cut the meat from the bones.

3. To make the sauce, put the pimentoes, 2 tablespoons of the reserved chicken stock (keep the remainder for soups or stocks), tomato purée and chutney into a saucepan and bring to the boil. Liquidize in a blender and set aside to cool.

4. Blend the cooled pimento mixture with the mayonnaise and season the sauce with salt and pepper.

5. Arrange the sliced chicken on a serving plate and cover it with the spiced mayonnaise. Arrange the pepper rings, tomato slices, if using, and watercress sprigs on the chicken. Serve this spicy dish with a variety of salads – such as Sunset stripe salad (page 67), Apricot and apple salad (page 60), green salad and potato salad sprinkled with fennel seeds.

Grilled Halibut with Mango Sauce

Per serving: 250 Calories, 1040 Kilojoules, 38g Protein, 5g Fat, 15g Carbohydrate, 2g Fibre, 195mg Sodium

1 tablespoon grated orange rind
juice of 2 oranges
2 bay leaves
1 small onion, peeled and chopped
freshly ground black pepper
4 halibut steaks, about 200g (7oz) each, washed and dried
oil for brushing
2 mangoes, peeled, stoned and halved
1 teaspoon cornflour
6 tablespoons plain unsweetened yogurt
sprigs of parsley, to garnish

Preparation time: 20 minutes, plus marinating
Cooking time: 20 minutes

1. Mix together the orange rind, orange juice, bay leaves and onion in a shallow dish and season with pepper. Place the fish in the marinade, cover and set aside for about 1 hour, turning the fish steaks once.

2. Lift the fish from the marinade and drain off the excess. Brush the fish and the grill rack with oil.

3. Cook the fish under a preheated hot grill for 10-12 minutes until it is just tender, turning it once.

4. Strain the marinade into a small saucepan. Press 1½ mangoes through a sieve and add to the marinade. Stir the cornflour into the yogurt. Stir the stabilized yogurt into the pan over moderate heat and heat to simmering point. Slice the remaining half mango.

5. Pour the sauce on to a serving dish, arrange the fish on it and garnish with the sliced mango and parsley sprigs. Serve with tiny new potatoes and fresh garden peas.

VEGETABLES AND SALADS

Split Pea and Ginger Dal

Per serving: 225 Calories, 940 Kilojoules, 15g Protein, 4g Fat,
35g Carbohydrate, 10g Fibre, 65mg Sodium

225g (8oz) yellow split peas, washed and drained
600ml (1 pint) chicken or vegetable stock
175g (6oz) cauliflower florets
1 tablespoon vegetable oil
½ teaspoon mustard seeds
½ teaspoon fennel seeds
1 teaspoon peeled and chopped root ginger
1 small onion, peeled and chopped
100g (4oz) button mushrooms, thinly sliced
salt
freshly ground black pepper
To garnish:
2 tablespoons chopped fresh coriander or parsley
lime slices
1 small onion, peeled and thinly sliced into rings

Preparation time: 15 minutes
Cooking time: about 1 hour

1. Put the split peas and stock into a saucepan, bring to the boil, cover and simmer for about 45 minutes or until the split peas are tender.
  Meanwhile, steam the cauliflower florets for 10 minutes until they are beginning to soften.
3. Heat the oil in a small saucepan and fry the mustard and fennel seeds and the ginger over moderate heat for 1 minute, stirring. Add the onion and fry for 3-4 minutes, stirring frequently.
4. Add the spiced onion mixture, the cauliflower and mushrooms to the pulses and season with salt and pepper. Simmer for 5 minutes for the flavours to blend.
5. Turn the dal into a heated serving dish. Sprinkle on the chopped herb and arrange the lime slices and onion rings on top. This spicy high-fibre dish makes a good accompaniment to grilled meats and poultry as well as curries.

Globe Artichokes with Minty Yogurt Dressing

Per serving: 110 Calories, 460 Kilojoules, 4g Protein,
6g Fat, 2g Carbohydrate, 2g Fibre, 75mg Sodium

4 large globe artichokes
3-4 tablespoons lemon juice
salt
1 tablespoon vegetable oil
sprigs of mint, to garnish
Dressing:
300ml (½ pint) Greek yogurt
½ teaspoon lemon rind
1 tablespoon lemon juice
1 tablespoon olive oil
10cm (4 inch) cucumber, peeled, seeded and grated
2 tablespoons chopped fresh mint
2 hard-boiled eggs, finely chopped
2 spring onions, trimmed and finely chopped

Preparation time: 40 minutes
Cooking time: 45 minutes

1. Have ready a bowl of water with 1 tablespoon of the lemon juice. Brush all the cut surfaces of the artichokes with lemon juice as you prepare them, and drop them into the acidulated water. Trim the artichoke stem level with the base of the leaves and, working all round each artichoke, cut off the 2 outside layers of leaves. Cut off the top third of the leaves.
2. Cook the artichokes in a pan of boiling, salted water with 1 tablespoon lemon juice added, for 35-45 minutes. When they are tender you will easily be able to pull away the outer leaves. Open out the centre of each artichoke, pull out the tight inner ring of pale leaves and, using a teaspoon, scrape out the prickly centre or 'choke'. Wash and drain the artichokes and leave them to cool for about 1 hour.
3. Mix all the ingredients for the dressing. Pour into a small bowl and garnish with sprigs of mint.

From the top: Split pea and ginger dal; Globe artichokes with minty yogurt dressing

*Clockwise from top left: Vegetable layer; Vegetable faggots;
Stir-fried mushrooms*

Vegetable Layer

Per serving: 315 Calories, 1310 Kilojoules, 35g Protein, 12g Fat,
20g Carbohydrate, 18g Fibre, 560mg Sodium

1kg (2lb) fresh spinach, washed and stalks removed
1 small cauliflower, cut into florets
salt
100g (4oz) low-fat hard cheese, grated
225g (8oz) tomatoes, skinned and sliced
freshly ground black pepper
2 tablespoons chopped fresh parsley
100g (4oz) button mushrooms, sliced
600ml (1 pint) plain unsweetened yogurt
3 eggs
pinch of grated nutmeg
25g (1oz) jumbo oats

Preparation time: 20 minutes
Cooking time: 45 minutes
Oven: 200° C, 400° F, Gas Mark 6

1. Cook the spinach, without added water, in a large saucepan over moderate heat for about 10 minutes, stirring frequently until the leaves have collapsed. Turn it into a colander and press it thoroughly to extract the moisture.
2. Cook the cauliflower in boiling salted water for about 10 minutes until the florets are beginning to soften.
3. Place the spinach in a shallow, greased baking dish. Sprinkle with 25g (1oz) of the cheese. Cover with the tomatoes, season with pepper and sprinkle on 1 tablespoon of the parsley, then cover with the sliced mushrooms and the cauliflower florets.
4. In a bowl beat the yogurt and beat in the eggs. Season with salt, pepper and nutmeg and stir in 50g (2oz) of the cheese. Pour the sauce over the vegetables. Mix the remaining cheese with the oats and sprinkle on top.
5. Place the dish on a baking sheet and cook in a preheated oven for 30 minutes or until the topping is brown and bubbling. Serve hot.

Vegetable Faggots

Per serving: 40 Calories, 170 Kilojoules, 2g Protein, Trace Fat,
8g Carbohydrate, 6g Fibre, 100mg Sodium

225g (8oz) carrots, cut into matchstick strips
1 heart tender celery, cut into matchstick strips
4 medium courgettes, cut into matchstick strips
225g (8oz) young French beans, topped, tailed and halved
1 small green pepper, cored, seeded and sliced into 8 thin rings
1 small red pepper, cored, seeded and sliced into 8 thin rings
1 tablespoon lemon juice
salt

Preparation time: 35 minutes
Cooking time: 10 minutes

1. Divide each vegetable into 4 – each person will have a bundle of carrots, celery, courgettes and beans. Push each bundle of carrots and celery into a green pepper ring and each bundle of courgettes and beans into a red pepper ring.
2. Place the lemon juice in the base of a steamer filled with boiling salted water and steam the bundles of carrots and celery for 10 minutes, or until they are just tender, and the courgettes and beans for about 8 minutes.
3. Arrange the bundles of vegetables on a large, heated serving dish and serve immediately.

Stir-Fried Mushrooms

Per serving: 230 Calories, 960 Kilojoules, 5g Protein, 18g Fat,
9g Carbohydrate, 4g Fibre, 10mg Sodium

225g (8oz) mange-touts, topped, tailed and cut diagonally into 4cm (1½ inch) slices
salt
3 tablespoons vegetable oil
1 garlic clove, peeled and crushed
225g (8oz) button mushrooms, sliced
50g (2oz) cashew nuts
Sauce:
2 tablespoons soy sauce
2 tablespoons dry sherry
5 tablespoons chicken stock
1 teaspoon clear honey
pinch of cayenne pepper

Preparation time: 20 minutes
Cooking time: 10 minutes

1. Cook the mange-tout slices in boiling salted water for 2 minutes. Drain them, then plunge them immediately into ice cold water to prevent further cooking and to preserve their colour. Drain and dry the mange-touts.
2. Mix all the sauce ingredients in a bowl.
3. Heat the oil in a heavy-based frying pan or a wok and stir-fry the garlic with a pinch of salt over high heat for 1 minute. Add the mange-tout slices and the button mushrooms and stir-fry them for 2 minutes.
4. Pour on the sauce, bring to the boil and cook for 2-3 minutes until the sauce has almost evaporated and the vegetables are just tender and glistening. Add the cashews and just heat through. Serve at once.

Nutty Croquettes

Per serving: 285 Calories, 1190 Kilojoules, 11g Protein, 12g Fat,
3g Carbohydrate, 8g Fibre, 90mg Sodium

350g (12oz) potatoes, peeled and sliced
350g (12oz) parsnips, peeled and sliced
salt
15g (½oz) soft margarine
1 small onion, peeled and chopped
freshly ground black pepper
pinch of grated nutmeg
1 teaspoon lemon juice
2 tablespoons chopped fresh parsley
2 eggs
3 tablespoons wholewheat flour
50g (2oz) raw peanuts, rubbed from skins and chopped
oil for brushing (optional)

Preparation time: 35 minutes
Cooking time: 35 minutes

1. Cook the potatoes and parsnips in boiling salted water for 15 minutes or until they are tender. Drain and mash the two together.
2. Melt the margarine in a small saucepan and fry the onion over moderate heat for 4 minutes, stirring occasionally.
3. Beat the onion into the potato and parsnip mixture, season with salt, pepper and nutmeg and stir in the lemon juice and 1 tablespoon of the parsley. Beat in 1 of the eggs and set aside to cool.
4. Beat the remaining egg. Shape the mixture into 8 flat cakes, toss them in flour Ⓕ and dip them in the beaten egg. Put the peanuts in a shallow bowl and press the vegetable cakes into them to coat thoroughly.
5. Fry the croquettes in a non-stick saucepan – or brush a pan lightly with oil – over moderate heat for about 5 minutes on each side. Serve hot with chilled Greek yogurt.
Ⓕ Open-freeze the croquettes before coating with egg and peanuts. Pack them in a rigid container and store for up to 3 months. Coat and cook the croquettes from frozen or after they have thawed.
Ⓜ Or microwave the croquettes, 4 at a time, for 4-8 minutes or until just soft, then continue from step 4.

Clockwise from the left: Asparagus with yogurt sauce; Stir-fried four; Apricot and apple salad

Asparagus with Yogurt Sauce

Per serving: 85 Calories, 350 Kilojoules, 12g Protein, 2g Fat, 3g Carbohydrate, 4g Fibre, 40mg Sodium

1kg (2¼lb) asparagus spears, trimmed and scraped
salt
2 hard-boiled eggs, separated and finely chopped
flat leaved parsley, to garnish
Sauce:
450ml (¾ pint) Greek yogurt
1 tablespoon lemon juice
2 tablespoons chopped fresh parsley

Preparation time: 20 minutes
Cooking time: about 10-20 minutes

1. Tie the asparagus into a bundle, using fine twine or soft string.
2. Cook the asparagus upright in a deep saucepan of boiling salted water reaching half-way up the stems, for 10-20 minutes, depending on the age and thickness of the asparagus. Untie the asparagus and drain it thoroughly.
3. To make the sauce, pour the yogurt into a small bowl, add the lemon juice, season with salt, and stir in the parsley.

4. Arrange the asparagus on a heated serving dish and garnish it with lines of chopped egg yolk and egg white and the parsley. Serve the sauce separately.

Apricot and Apple Salad

Per serving: 360 Calories, 1510 Kilojoules, 4g Protein, 21g Fat, 40g Carbohydrate, 14g Fibre, 60mg Sodium

175g (6oz) dried apricot halves
200ml (7fl oz) cloudy apple juice
3 dessert apples, cored and thinly sliced
3 tender celery sticks, thinly sliced
3 tablespoons walnut halves
celery leaves, to garnish
Dressing:
3 tablespoons vegetable oil
3 tablespoons cloudy apple juice
2 tablespoons pumpkin seeds
salt
freshly ground black pepper

Preparation time: 15 minutes, plus soaking

1. Soak the dried apricots in the apple juice for about 2 hours. Stir in the sliced apples, celery and walnuts.
2. Mix together the dressing ingredients.
3. Pour the dressing over the fruit mixture and toss well.
4. Spoon the salad on to a serving dish and garnish with celery leaves. This colourful, crunchy and high-in-fibre salad is particularly good with cold game and poultry.

Stir-Fried Four

Per serving: 220 Calories, 920 Kilojoules, 7g Protein, 18g Fat,
6g Carbohydrate, 4g Fibre, 170mg Sodium

225g (8oz) broccoli spears, cut diagonally into 2.5cm
(1 inch) slices
4 tender celery sticks, sliced into matchstick strips
salt
3 tablespoons vegetable oil
1 garlic clove, peeled and finely chopped
2 small red peppers, cored, seeded and thinly sliced
100g (4oz) fresh bean shoots
150ml ($\frac{1}{4}$pint) chicken stock
2 tablespoons soy sauce
3 tablespoons dry white wine
1 teaspoon sugar
Omelette strips:
2 eggs
2 tablespoons water
$\frac{1}{2}$ teaspoon soy sauce
1 tablespoon vegetable oil

Preparation time: 20 minutes
Cooking time: 15 minutes

1. Blanch the broccoli and celery in a saucepan of boiling, salted water for 2 minutes. Drain, then plunge them at once into ice-cold water, then drain again and dry.
2. Heat the oil in a heavy-based frying pan or a wok, stir-fry the garlic over high heat for 1 minute, then discard it. (This is the stir-frying equivalent of rubbing a salad bowl with a cut garlic clove.)
3. Place the broccoli, celery and peppers in the frying pan and stir-fry for 2 minutes. Add the bean shoots and stir-fry for a further 2 minutes. Add the chicken stock, season with salt, stir and boil for 2 minutes. Add the soy sauce, white wine and sugar and boil for 1 minute, stirring.
4. To make the omelette, beat the eggs with the water and soy sauce and season with salt. Heat the oil in an omelette pan or small frying-pan, pour in the egg mixture, tilt the pan and cook over moderate heat for 3-4 minutes until the omelette is set. Slide it on to a plate and cut it into 1cm ($\frac{1}{2}$ inch) strips.
5. Turn the vegetables into a heated serving dish and arrange the omelette strips in a criss-cross pattern on top.

Spinach Parcels in Lemon Sauce

Per serving: 215 Calories, 890 Kilojoules, 10g Protein, 16g Fat,
9g Carbohydrate, 9g Fibre, 170mg Sodium

16 large spinach leaves, stalks removed
2 tablespoons vegetable oil
6 spring onions, trimmed and finely chopped
2 small tender celery sticks, finely chopped
1 medium carrot, finely chopped
100g (4oz) mushrooms, chopped
75g (3oz) cooked brown rice
2 tablespoons blanched chopped almonds
1 tablespoon chopped fresh parsley
salt
freshly ground black pepper
$\frac{1}{4}$ teaspoon lemon rind
2 tablespoons chicken or vegetable stock
Sauce:
300ml ($\frac{1}{2}$ pint) chicken or vegetable stock
2 bay leaves
2 egg yolks
2 tablespoons lemon juice

Preparation time: 30 minutes
Cooking time: 30 minutes

1. Blanch the spinach leaves in boiling water for 1 minute. Drain them, plunge them at once into ice-cold water to prevent further cooking, then drain them again. Pat dry with paper towels.
2. Heat the oil in a frying pan and fry the onion, celery and carrot over moderate heat for 3 minutes. Stir in the mushrooms, cook for 2 minutes, then add the rice, almonds and parsley. Season with salt and pepper, stir in the lemon rind and stock and simmer for 3 minutes until the mixture is well blended but still moist.
3. Place the spinach leaves flat on a working surface. Spoon the vegetable filling into the centre of each leaf. Turn up the base of each leaf, fold over the sides then fold down the top to enclose the filling.
4. Pour the stock into the base of a steaming pan or a saucepan, add the bay leaves and fit on the steamer. Bring the stock to the boil, place the spinach parcels, join sides down, on the steamer, cover and steam for 10 minutes. Keep the spinach parcels warm while you make the sauce.
5. Discard the bay leaves. Beat the egg yolks with 3 tablespoons of the stock, beat in the lemon juice and season with salt and pepper. Pour the mixture into the remaining stock and heat very gently for 3-4 minutes, stirring constantly. Do not let the sauce boil, or the yolks will scramble.
6. Pour the sauce on to a heated serving dish and arrange the spinach parcels on it.

Layered Vegetable Terrine

Per small serving: 165 Calories, 690 Kilojoules, 5g Protein, 14g Fat, 5g Carbohydrate, 3g Fibre, 150mg Sodium

Serves 8-10
450g (1lb) carrots, cut into 'pencil' strips
225g (8oz) young French beans, topped and tailed
225g (8oz) small, white turnips, cut into matchstick strips
225g (8oz) asparagus spears, trimmed and scraped
600ml (1 pint) chicken or vegetable stock
4-6 tablespoons aspic crystals
2 tablespoons sherry
1 teaspoon lemon juice
salt
freshly ground black pepper
1 teaspoon Dijon mustard
150ml ($\frac{1}{4}$ pint) mayonnaise
150ml ($\frac{1}{4}$ pint) plain unsweetened yogurt
4 small hard-boiled eggs
sprigs of dill, to garnish

Preparation time: 1 hour, plus chilling
Cooking time: about 30 minutes

1. Steam the vegetables over the boiling stock, each type separately, until they are just tender. Drain them, reserving the stock, and plunge at once into separate bowls of ice-cold water. When they are cold, drain and dry them.
2. Make the hot stock up to 600ml (1 pint) and mix in the aspic crystals and stir until they are dissolved. Set aside to cool. Stir in the sherry and lemon juice, season with salt and pepper and remove and reserve 5 tablespoons of the solution to glaze the top of the terrine. Stir the mustard, mayonnaise and yogurt into the aspic and beat until the mixture is smooth and well blended.
3. Rinse a 1.2 litre (2 pint) loaf tin with cold water and drain it thoroughly. Pour a very thin layer of the aspic mixture into the tin. Make a layer of half the carrots, the strips running lengthways along the tin, then half the beans, turnips and asparagus. Place the eggs in the centre and cover them with the remaining vegetables in the reverse order. (The vegetables will settle around the eggs.)
4. Pour on the aspic mixture, tapping the tin so that it fills up all the crevices. Cover the tin with foil and chill in the refrigerator for 3-4 hours.
5. Run a knife around the tin to loosen the terrine, then invert it on to a serving dish. Arrange a pattern of herb sprigs on top. Melt the reserved aspic solution and brush it over the terrine. Chill for about 1 hour to set the glaze.
6. Serve the terrine, sliced, with a selection of salads for a summer buffet, or with wholemeal bread as a first course.

Spring Vegetables in Curry Sauce

Per serving: 120 Calories, 500 Kilojoules, 5g Protein, 6g Fat, 13g Carbohydrate, 8g Fibre, 135mg Sodium

1 small cauliflower, cut into florets
225g (8oz) carrots, thinly sliced
225g (8oz) shelled broad beans
225g (8oz) young French beans, topped, tailed and halved
450ml ($\frac{3}{4}$ pint) chicken or vegetable stock
1 lemon, quartered, to serve
Sauce:
25g (1oz) soft margarine
1 small onion, peeled and chopped
2 teaspoons curry powder
1 teaspoon curry paste
1 tablespoon wholewheat flour
150ml ($\frac{1}{4}$ pint) Greek yogurt
1 teaspoon lemon juice
salt
freshly ground black pepper

Preparation time: 20 minutes
Cooking time: 25 minutes

1. Steam the vegetables in a covered pan over the stock for 12 minutes, or simmer them in the stock for 9-10 minutes until they are just tender. Drain the vegetables and reserve the stock.
2. To make the sauce, melt the margarine in a saucepan and fry the onion over moderate heat for 3 minutes, stirring occasionally. Stir in the curry powder and curry paste and cook for 1 minute. Stir in the flour and cook for 2 minutes. Measure 275ml (9fl oz) of the reserved stock and gradually pour it on to the curry mixture, stirring constantly. Gradually stir in the yogurt, then add the lemon juice and season with salt and pepper. Bring the sauce slowly to the boil and simmer for 2-3 minutes.
3. Place the vegetables in a warmed serving dish and stir in the sauce. Serve garnished with the lemon wedges.

Clockwise from top left: Layered vegetable terrine;
Spring vegetables in curry sauce;
Chick pea and red pepper salad

Chick Pea and Red Pepper Salad

Preparation time: 15 minutes, plus soaking
Cooking time: about 2 hours

Per serving: 270 Calories, 1140 Kilojoules, 10g Protein, 15g Fat, 24g Carbohydrate, 8g Fibre, 360mg Sodium

175g (6oz) chick peas, soaked overnight and drained
2 red peppers
12 black olives
2 tablespoons chopped fresh coriander, or parsley
sprigs of parsley, to garnish
Dressing:
3 tablespoons vegetable oil
$\frac{1}{2}$ teaspoon orange rind
2 tablespoons orange juice
1 garlic clove, peeled and crushed
salt
freshly ground black pepper

1. Cook the chick peas in boiling unsalted water for 2 hours, or until they are tender. The actual length of the cooking time will depend on the 'age' of the pulses – how long they have been on the shelf. Drain the chick peas, run hot water over them and drain them again.
2. Place the red peppers on a grill rack and cook them under moderate heat for about 20 minutes, turning them frequently until the skins are black and blistered. Hold the peppers under cold water then, using a small, sharp knife, peel off the skins. Halve the peppers, remove the core and seeds and thinly slice them.
3. Mix the dressing ingredients.
4. Toss the chick peas in the dressing while they are still hot. Set aside to cool. Stir in the peppers and olives and half the parsley. Turn the salad into a serving dish and sprinkle on the remaining parsley and garnish with the sprigs of parsley.

Spiced Rice and Lentil Kedgeree

Per serving: **560** Calories, **2380** Kilojoules, 22g Protein, 16g Fat, 88g Carbohydrate, 12g Fibre, 70mg Sodium

225g (8oz) brown continental lentils, soaked and drained
3 tablespoons vegetable oil
1 medium onion, peeled and chopped
2 garlic cloves, peeled and finely chopped
1 teaspoon ground cumin
$\frac{1}{2}$ teaspoon ground turmeric
$\frac{1}{2}$ teaspoon ground coriander
large pinch of cayenne pepper
1 tablespoon finely chopped peeled root ginger
225g (8oz) brown rice, washed and drained
1 litre ($1\frac{3}{4}$ pints) chicken stock
salt
freshly ground black pepper
2 tablespoons chopped fresh coriander or parsley
To serve:
1 small onion, peeled and thinly sliced into rings
2 medium bananas, sliced
2 tablespoons lemon juice
2 hard-boiled eggs, quartered
sprigs of parsley

Preparation time: 20 minutes
Cooking time: about 55 minutes

1. Cook the lentils in boiling unsalted water for 10 minutes. Drain the lentils.
2. Heat the oil in a large frying pan and fry the onion over moderate heat for 3 minutes, stirring once or twice. Stir in the garlic, cumin, turmeric, coriander, cayenne and ginger and cook for 1 minute, then stir in the partly cooked lentils and the rice. Pour on the stock, stir well and bring the mixture to the boil.
3. Cover the pan and simmer for 45 minutes until the rice and lentils are tender. Season with salt and pepper and, if there is any liquid remaining, evaporate it by boiling with the pan uncovered for a few minutes. Stir in the chopped herb.
4. Turn the kedgeree into a heated serving dish. Scatter the onion rings on top and serve the dish with banana slices tossed in lemon juice and the hard-boiled egg quarters. Garnish with sprigs of parsley and serve with a green salad.

From the left: Spiced rice and lentil kedgeree;
Burghul tomato cases

Burghul Tomato Cases

Per serving: **175** Calories, **730** Kilojoules, 5g Protein, 14g Fat, 11g Carbohydrate, 6g Fibre, 15mg Sodium

50g (2oz) fine cracked wheat (burghul)
$\frac{1}{4}$ teaspoon salt
2 tablespoons lemon juice
8 large tomatoes
2 spring onions, trimmed and finely chopped
8 tablespoons chopped fresh coriander or parsley
2 tablespoons chopped fresh mint
3 tablespoons olive oil
freshly ground black pepper
To garnish:
salad leaves or vine leaves
sprigs of mint
thin slices of lemon

Baked Aubergines

Per serving: 220 Calories, 915 Kilojoules, 10g Protein, 10g Fat, 26g Carbohydrate, 8g Fibre, 440mg Sodium

4 small aubergines
salt
2 tablespoons vegetable oil, plus extra for brushing
1 small onion, peeled and chopped
1 garlic clove, peeled and crushed
1 red pepper, cored, seeded and chopped
2 courgettes, trimmed and chopped
2 tablespoons chopped fresh mint
4 tablespoons cooked brown rice
8 black olives, stoned and chopped
4 tablespoons chopped cashew nuts
freshly ground black pepper
75g (3oz) Ricotta cheese
6 tablespoons wholewheat breadcrumbs
3 large tomatoes, thinly sliced
$\frac{1}{2}$ teaspoon dried oregano

Preparation time: 25 minutes, plus draining
Cooking time: 45 minutes
Oven: 190° C, 375° F, Gas Mark 5

1. Halve the aubergines lengthways and scoop out the flesh, taking care not to pierce the walls. Chop the flesh and put it into a colander. Sprinkle the chopped aubergine and the 'shells' with salt and stand the shells upside-down on a plate. Leave to drain for at least 30 minutes. Rinse the aubergine under cold running water and dry the flesh and the shells.
2. Heat the oil in a frying pan and fry the onion over moderate heat for 3 minutes, stirring once or twice. Stir in the garlic, red pepper, courgettes and chopped aubergine and cook for 5 minutes, stirring frequently. Stir in the mint, rice, olives and nuts and cook for 2-3 minutes. Season with salt and pepper.
3. Spoon the vegetable mixture into the aubergine cases and place them in a shallow, greased baking dish. In a small bowl, mix the cheese and breadcrumbs with a fork. Sprinkle the topping over the aubergines, arrange the tomato slices on top, brush them with oil and sprinkle with the oregano.
4. Bake the aubergines in a preheated oven for 20-25 minutes, until the cheese topping is crisp and brown. Serve hot or cold with new potatoes and a salad.

Preparation time: 15 minutes, plus soaking and standing

1. Soak the cracked wheat in water for 15 minutes. Drain it, tip it into a clean tea towel and wring it tightly to remove excess moisture.
2. Turn the cracked wheat into a bowl, sprinkle it with the salt and lemon juice and set aside for 1 hour.
3. Cut the tops from the tomatoes and, if necessary, cut a very thin slice from the base so that they stand evenly. Using a teaspoon or vegetable baller, scoop out the flesh and seeds, chop and set aside. Make a pad with a paper towel and dry the tomato 'cases'.
4. Stir the chopped tomato, spring onion, chopped herbs and olive oil into the cracked wheat and season it with pepper. Taste and adjust the seasoning if necessary.
5. Spoon the salad into the tomato cases, shaping it up into a dome. Place the tomato cases on a serving dish lined with salad leaves or vine leaves and garnish them with sprigs of mint and slices of lemon.

Clockwise from the left: Red and green salad with cheese dressing; Sunset stripe salad; Celeriac and carrot remoulade

Red and Green Salad with Cheese Dressing

Per serving: 300 Calories, 1250 Kilojoules, 8g Protein, 26g Fat, 8g Carbohydrate, 4g Fibre, 260mg Sodium

225g (8oz) courgettes, trimmed and thinly sliced
100g (4oz) button mushrooms, thinly sliced
2 tablespoons finely snipped fresh chives
4 large tomatoes, thinly sliced
$\frac{1}{2}$ cucumber, thinly sliced
1 red pepper, cored, seeded and thinly sliced into rings
Dressing:
6 tablespoons vegetable oil
3 tablespoons red wine vinegar
salt
freshly ground black pepper
pinch of mustard powder
5 tablespoons buttermilk, or plain unsweetened yogurt
50g (2oz) Roquefort cheese, crumbled
50g (2oz) Ricotta cheese, crumbled

Preparation time: 30 minutes, plus marinating

1. Mix together the oil and vinegar and season with salt, pepper and mustard.
2. Put the courgettes and the mushrooms in separate small dishes and divide the dressing between them. Stir the chives into the courgettes. Set aside for at least 1 hour.
3. Arrange the tomatoes in a ring around the outside of a serving dish. Arrange the cucumber slices in a ring overlapping the tomatoes and then arrange a circle of red peppers. Drain the courgettes and make a ring with them, finally, drain the mushrooms and arrange them in the centre.
4. Stir the buttermilk or yogurt into the reserved dressing and stir in the cheeses. Spoon the dressing into the centre of the salad.

Variation:
For a quicker version of this salad, mix all the dressing ingredients together, toss in the courgettes and mushrooms and set aside for about 1 hour. Arrange the tomatoes and cucumber on a bed of salad leaves with the pepper rings in the middle and spoon the mixed salad in the centre.

66

Sunset Stripe Salad

Per serving: 300 Calories, 1250 Kilojoules, 12g Protein, 16g Fat, 30g Carbohydrate, 15g Fibre, 90mg Sodium

Always fast-boil dried red kidney beans for the first 15-20 minutes of cooking to dispel harmful toxins, then lower the heat to a gentle boil.

175g (6oz) dried red kidney beans, soaked overnight and drained
few stalks of parsley
1 small onion, peeled and halved
175g (6oz) red cabbage, coarsely shredded
2 small heads fennel, very thinly sliced into rings
2 oranges, segmented
To garnish:
sprigs of parsley
tomato roses (below)
Dressing:
4 tablespoons vegetable oil
$\frac{1}{2}$ teaspoon grated orange rind
4 tablespoons orange juice
$\frac{1}{2}$ teaspoon fennel seeds, lightly crushed
1 garlic clove, peeled and halved
large pinch of mustard powder
salt
freshly ground black pepper

*Preparation time: 25 minutes, plus soaking and standing
Cooking time: about 1$\frac{1}{4}$ hours*

1. Cook the kidney beans in boiling unsalted water with the parsley stalks and onion for about 1$\frac{1}{4}$ hours, or until they are just tender. Drain them into a colander, discard the flavourings, run hot water through the beans and drain them again.
2. Meanwhile, mix the dressing ingredients and set aside for about 1 hour. Strain the dressing.
3. Toss the beans in the dressing while they are still hot. Set aside to cool.
4. In a glass dish, make a layer of the red cabbage, then the fennel, then the orange segments, and cover them with the beans. Cover and set aside for at least 1 hour. Make a pad of parsley sprigs and arrange it on the salad and place the tomato rose on top.

Tomato Roses

Choose a firm, slightly under-ripe tomato. Starting at the top and using a sharp knife, peel off a continuous spiral of skin about 1cm ($\frac{1}{2}$ inch) wide. With the skin outside, curl the strip into a tight spiral. From the top, arranged on a 'pad' of watercress leaves, it will look mighty like a rose!

Celeriac and Carrot Remoulade

Per serving: 165 Calories, 690 Kilojoules, 5g Protein, 15g Fat, 4g Carbohydrate, 5g Fibre, 160mg Sodium

1 celeriac root, about 225g (8oz), scrubbed and sliced into matchstick strips
2 tablespoons lemon juice
225g (8oz) carrots, sliced into matchstick strips
salt
To garnish:
1 hard-boiled egg, separated
snipped fresh chives
carrot curls (below)
Dressing:
4 tablespoons mayonnaise
150ml ($\frac{1}{4}$ pint) Greek yogurt
1 garlic clove, peeled and crushed
1 tablespoon chopped fresh parsley
1 tablespoon finely snipped fresh chives
$\frac{1}{2}$ teaspoon mustard powder
1 pinch of cayenne pepper
1 hard-boiled egg, finely chopped

*Preparation time: 20 minutes, plus cooling
Cooking time: 10 minutes*

1. Drop the celeriac strips as you cut them into bowl of water acidulated with 1 tablespoon of the lemon juice. This will help to preserve their creamy colour.
2. Partly cook the celeriac and carrot strips for 5-8 minutes in boiling salted water with the remaining lemon juice. Drain, dry and cool the vegetables. (Reserve the flavoured stock for soup or a casserole.)
3. Mix the dressing ingredients. Taste and adjust the seasoning if necessary.
4. Toss the celeriac and carrots in the dressing and spoon the salad on to a serving dish. Sieve the egg yolk and arrange it in the centre of the salad. Chop the white finely and place it on top, then arrange the chopped chives around the edge and garnish with carrot curls.

Carrot Curls

Choose large carrots and peel or scrub them. Using a potato peeler, pare thin strips from the length of each carrot. Roll up the strips, secure them on wooden cocktail sticks and place them in ice-cold water for about 1 hour. Drain and dry the carrot curls and remove the sticks. Unroll 3 carrot curls and place them one on top of the other in opposite directions. They will spring back to form a rose.

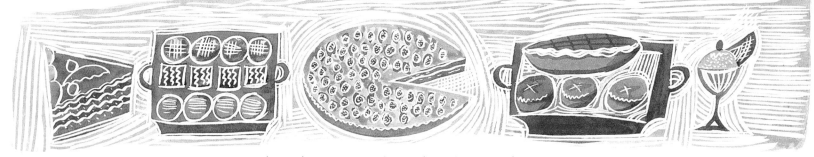

DESSERTS, CAKES AND BISCUITS

Cherry Cobbler

Per serving: 320 Calories, 1340 Kilojoules, 8g Protein, 9g Fat,
56g Carbohydrate, 6g Fibre, 100mg Sodium

Serves 6
2 tablespoons orange juice
40g (1½oz) light muscovado sugar
1 bay leaf
900g (2lb) dessert cherries, stoned
chilled Greek yogurt, to serve
Topping:
225g (8oz) wholewheat self-raising flour
1 teaspoon baking powder
salt
pinch of grated nutmeg
50g (2oz) soft margarine
40g (1½oz) demerara sugar, plus extra for sprinkling
1 teaspoon grated orange rind
2 tablespoons orange juice
1 egg, beaten
100ml (3½fl oz) plain unsweetened yogurt
milk, for brushing

Preparation time: 25 minutes
Cooking time: 50 minutes
Oven: 200°C, 400°F, Gas Mark 6

1. Put the orange juice, muscovado sugar and bay leaf into a frying pan and stir over low heat until the sugar has dissolved. Add the cherries, reserving a few for decoration, and simmer for about 10 minutes, shaking the pan frequently, until they are just tender. Turn the cherries into a baking dish and discard the bay leaf. Set aside to cool.
2. Sift the flour, baking powder, salt and nutmeg into a mixing bowl and tip in any bran remaining in the sieve. Rub in the margarine with a fork, stir in the demerara sugar and orange rind, sprinkle on the orange juice and stir in the beaten egg and yogurt. Shape the mixture into a ball, and knead the dough lightly until it is smooth.
3. Roll out the dough on a lightly floured board until it is

2cm (¾ inch) thick. Use a heart-shaped biscuit cutter to cut out the dough. Arrange the scone shapes over the fruit, brush with milk and sprinkle on a little sugar.
4. Bake the pudding in a preheated oven for 35 minutes or until the topping is well risen and golden brown. Serve hot with chilled Greek yogurt.

Green Fruit Pudding

Per serving: 190 Calories, 795 Kilojoules, 6g Protein, 2g Fat,
40g Carbohydrate, 9g Fibre, 275mg Sodium

Serves 6
10 large thin slices wholewheat bread, crusts removed
4-5 tablespoons clear honey
350g (12oz) gooseberries, topped and tailed
350g (12oz) greengages, stoned and roughly chopped
2 small cooking apples, peeled, cored and thinly sliced
few mint or scented geranium leaves, to decorate
300ml (½ pint) Greek yogurt, beaten, to serve

Preparation time: 25 minutes, plus chilling overnight
Cooking time: 20 minutes

1. Line a greased 1.2 litre (2 pint) bowl or pudding basin with bread, cutting and fitting it to ensure there are no gaps.
2. Melt the honey in a large frying pan over low heat. Add all the fruit, reserving a few gooseberries for decoration. Shake the pan and simmer for about 12-15 minutes, until the fruit is quite tender.
3. Spoon a little of the juice over the bread, then pour in the fruit to fill the lined bowl. Cover the top with the remaining bread, taking great care to fit it closely and neatly around the rim. Cover the bowl with a saucer that just fits inside the rim, then weight it down with a large filled can or something equally large and heavy.
4. Chill the pudding overnight. Run a knife around the edge and unmould it on to a flat serving plate. Decorate the pudding with the reserved gooseberries and leaves and serve it cold, cut into wedges, with chilled Greek yogurt.

From the top: Cherry cobbler; Green fruit pudding

Baked Orange Flowers

Per serving: 245 Calories, 1030 Kilojoules, 4g Protein, 8g Fat, 38g Carbohydrate, 8g Fibre, 15mg Sodium

4 large thin skinned oranges
4 tablespoons currants
4 tablespoons chopped blanched almonds
4 tablespoons clear honey
2 tablespoons dark rum (optional)
2 teaspoons lemon juice
2 tablespoons water

Preparation time: 20 minutes
Cooking time: 25 minutes
Oven: 180°C, 350°F, Gas Mark 4

1. Using a sharp knife and working from the top, divide the peel of each orange into 8 'petals' without cutting through to the base. Gently pull away the peel and tuck the end of each 'petal' in between the base of the orange and the attached peel. Carefully open out each orange from the centre to make a cavity.
2. Mix together the currants and almonds and pack the mixture into the orange centres.
3. Put the honey, rum, if using, lemon juice and water into a small saucepan and heat gently to melt the honey.
4. Place each orange in the centre of a 25cm (10 inch) piece of greased aluminium foil. Pour the honey solution into the centres of the oranges and closely fold over the foil to make steamproof parcels.
5. Bake the oranges in a preheated oven for 20 minutes. Unwrap the oranges and serve them hot or cold with plain unsweetened yogurt.

Blueberry Creams

Per serving: 165 Calories, 685 Kilojoules, 4g Protein, Trace Fat, 26g Carbohydrate, 2g Fibre, 30mg Sodium

3 tablespoons clear honey
2 tablespoons orange juice
1½ teaspoons grated orange rind
450g (1lb) blueberries
3 tablespoons wholewheat flour
150ml (¼ pint) plain unsweetened yogurt
4 small mint sprigs, to decorate

Preparation time: 20 minutes, plus cooling
Cooking time: 20 minutes

1. Put the honey, orange juice and orange rind into a saucepan and stir over low heat until the honey has melted. Add the blueberries and simmer for 10 minutes, or until the fruit is tender. Liquidize the fruit and juice in a blender, or rub them through a sieve.
2. Stir a little of the purée into the flour to make a smooth paste. Stir in the remainder of the purée, return it to the pan and stir over medium heat until the purée thickens. Simmer for 3 minutes. Cool slightly. Ⓕ
3. Divide the fruit purée between 4 individual serving glasses and chill in the refrigerator.
4. Stir the yogurt through the blueberry creams and decorate with the mint sprigs. Serve chilled.
Ⓕ This dessert freezes well. Pack it in a sealed polythene box and freeze for up to 6 months. Thaw for 6 hours at room temperature or overnight in the refrigerator, then spoon it into the glasses and top with the yogurt.

Gooseberry Oat Flan

Per serving: 390 Calories, 1630 Kilojoules, 13g Protein, 17g Fat, 50g Carbohydrate, 8g Fibre, 500mg Sodium

Serves 6
225g (8oz) cottage cheese
50g (2oz) porridge oats
1 teaspoon grated lemon rind
½ teaspoon ground cinnamon
2 bananas, peeled and mashed
450g (1lb) gooseberries, topped and tailed
3 tablespoons demerara sugar
Pastry:
175g (6oz) wholewheat flour
2 teaspoons baking powder
salt
½ teaspoon ground cinnamon
50g (2oz) porridge oats
100g (4oz) soft margarine
3 tablespoons plain unsweetened yogurt

Preparation time: 25 minutes
Cooking time: 40 minutes
Oven: 190°C, 375°F, Gas Mark 5

1. To make the pastry, sift together the flour, baking powder, salt and cinnamon in a mixing bowl; tip in any bran remaining in the sieve and stir in the oats. Using a fork beat in the margarine and stir in the yogurt. Form the mixture into a ball and knead it lightly until it is smooth.
2. Roll out the pastry on a lightly floured board until it is 5mm (¼ inch) thick and use it to line a 20cm (8 inch) greased flan ring placed on a greased baking sheet. Prick all over the base with a fork. Ⓕ
3. Mix together the cottage cheese, oats, lemon rind, cinnamon and bananas and spread the mixture over the pastry case. Arrange the gooseberries in rings on top and sprinkle on the sugar.
4. Bake in a preheated oven for 35–40 minutes until the pastry case is well browned. Serve warm or cold.
Ⓕ Bake the pastry case 'blind' for 20 minutes, then cool and freeze it for up to 6 months. Thaw the pastry, fill it with the cheese mixture and fruit and bake for 25 minutes.

From the left: Baked orange flowers; Blueberry creams

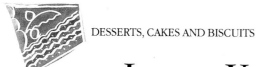

Lemon Yogurt Syllabub

Per serving: 120 Calories, 490 Kilojoules, 4g Protein, 4g Fat,
15g Carbohydrate, Trace Fibre, 60mg Sodium

450ml (¾ pint) Greek yogurt
3 tablespoons clear honey
grated rind of 1 lemon
juice of 2 lemons
2 tablespoons sherry
fresh fruit, to decorate (see method)

Preparation time: 15 minutes

1. Whisk the yogurt in a bowl, then beat in the honey and lemon rind. Gradually add the lemon juice and sherry, stirring all the time.
2. Divide the syllabub between individual serving glasses. This dessert is particularly delicious if served topped with few fresh raspberries, strawberries or blackberries, or decorate each glass with a thin slice of lemon and a sprig of mint. Serve chilled.

Sunrise Fruit Salad

Per serving: 130 Calories, 550 Kilojoules, 3g Protein, 0 Fat,
29g Carbohydrate, 13g Fibre, 25mg Sodium

Serves 6
3 oranges, peeled and very thinly sliced
4 tablespoons orange liqueur
225g (8oz) whole dried apricots
juice of 2 oranges
6 tablespoons water
2 scented geranium leaves or 1 bay leaf
225g (8oz) blackberries, hulled

Preparation time: 20 minutes, plus macerating
Cooking time: 20 minutes

1. Place the orange slices in a shallow dish, pour on the liqueur, cover, and set aside for at least 2 hours.
2. Soak the apricots in the orange juice and water for 2 hours. Simmer the fruit with the geranium leaves or bay leaf for 20 minutes. Set aside to cool. Discard the geranium leaves or bay leaf.
3. Make a ring of the orange slices around the edge of a serving dish. Spoon the apricots into the centre. Make a ring of the blackberries to divide the two orange coloured fruits. Mix together the orange liqueur and the apricot liquid and pour the dressing over the fruit salad. Serve cold, but not chilled with a little Greek yogurt, if wished.

Cassis Fruit Salad

Per small serving: 135 Calories, 565 Kilojoules, 3g Protein, 3g Fat,
22g Carbohydrate, 7g Fibre, Trace Salt

Serves 4-6
3 tablespoons orange juice
4 tablespoons Crème de Cassis
3 tablespoons clear honey
450g (1lb) black dessert cherries, stoned
225g (8oz) ripe blackcurrants trimmed and 'tailed'
225g (8oz) loganberries or raspberries, hulled
2 tablespoons pine nuts

Preparation time: 30 minutes, plus macerating

1. Mix together the orange juice, Crème de Cassis and honey and stir until the honey has dissolved.
2. Mix the cherries, blackcurrants and berries. Pour over the Cassis mixture, stir well, cover and chill for at least 3 hours. Some of the juice will be drawn from the fruit to make a tangy dressing. Scatter on the pine nuts just before serving. Serve chilled, with plain unsweetened yogurt.

Fresh Fruit Platter

Per serving: 130 Calories, 550 Kilojoules, 2g Protein, 0 Fat,
34g Carbohydrate, 4g Fibre, 10mg Sodium

4 fresh black figs, quartered
2 mangoes, peeled, stoned and sliced
½ small watermelon, peeled and thinly sliced
225g (8oz) fresh dates
vine leaves or scented geranium leaves, to serve
(optional)
Sauce:
300ml (½ pint) Greek yogurt
4 teaspoons dark muscovado sugar

Preparation time: 20 minutes, plus chilling

1. To make the sauce, stir the yogurt and place it in a small serving bowl. Sprinkle the sugar evenly over the top and chill for at least 1 hour.
2. Line 4 individual serving plates with vine leaves or scented geranium leaves, if wished. Divide the figs, mango slices, watermelon and dates between the 4 plates. Serve the yogurt sauce separately.

Clockwise from top left: Lemon yogurt syllabub;
Cassis fruit salad; Fresh fruit platter; Sunrise fruit salad

Clockwise from top left: Apple ring with spiced apricot sauce; Baked cranberry pears; Rice and raisin pudding

Apple Ring with Spiced Apricot Sauce

Per serving: 180 Calories, 760 Kilojoules, 8g Protein, 2g Fat, 33g Carbohydrate, 11g Fibre, 65mg Sodium

Serves 6
450g (1lb) cooking apples, peeled, cored and chopped
150ml ($\frac{1}{4}$ pint) water
grated rind and juice of 1 lemon
2 cloves
25g (1oz) powdered gelatine
2 eggs, separated
40g (1$\frac{1}{2}$oz) light muscovado sugar
150ml ($\frac{1}{4}$ pint) plain unsweetened yogurt
Sauce:
100g (4oz) dried apricots
300ml ($\frac{1}{2}$ pint) water
rind and juice of $\frac{1}{2}$ lemon
$\frac{1}{2}$ cinnamon stick
1 clove
1 tablespoon apricot liqueur (optional)

Preparation time: 30 minutes, plus soaking and setting
Cooking time: 40 minutes

1. Place the apples in a saucepan with the water, lemon rind and cloves. Bring to the boil and simmer for about 10 minutes or until the apples are tender. Discard the cloves.
2. Sprinkle the gelatine on to the lemon juice and stir over hot water until the gelatine has dissolved. Pour the gelatine solution into the apple mixture and liquidize in a blender. Set aside to cool.
3. Whisk the egg yolks with the sugar until the mixture is light and fluffy. Stir the egg mixture and the yogurt into the thickening apple purée. Whisk the egg whites until they are stiff and fold them into the purée.
4. Rinse a 1.2 litre (2 pint) ring mould with cold water. Pour in the apple mixture and chill for 3 hours until the purée has set.
5. To make the sauce, soak the apricots in the water for 2 hours. Pour into a saucepan, add the lemon rind, lemon juice, cinnamon and clove, bring to the boil and simmer for 20 minutes. Remove the cinnamon and clove and liquidize the apricots in a blender, or rub them through a sieve. Stir in the liqueur if using. Set aside to cool. Turn the apple mould on to a serving dish, drizzle a little of the sauce over it and serve the rest separately.

Baked Cranberry Pears

Per serving: 160 Calories, 675 Kilojoules, 2g Protein, 3g Fat, 28g Carbohydrate, 6g Fibre, 15mg Sodium

4 large, ripe dessert pears, peeled but with the stalks in place
225g (8oz) cranberries, thawed, if frozen
1 tablespoon chopped Brazil nuts or hazelnuts
3 tablespoons clear honey
150ml ($\frac{1}{4}$ pint) white wine
1 tablespoon grenadine syrup
sprigs of mint, to decorate

Preparation time: 20 minutes
Cooking time: 40 minutes
Oven: 200°C, 400°F, Gas Mark 6

1. Working from the base and using a small teaspoon, scoop out the pear cores. Take 2 tablespoons of the cranberries, chop and mix with the nuts and 1 tablespoon of the honey. Press the mixture into the pear cavities.
2. Place the remaining cranberries, honey, wine and grenadine syrup in a flameproof dish and bring to the boil over moderate heat. Simmer for 5 minutes. Stand the pears upright in the dish and spoon the wine over them.
3. Cover the dish lightly with foil and cook in a preheated oven for 30 minutes, basting the pears with the wine once or twice. Decorate each pear with a sprig of mint and serve hot or cold.

Rice and Raisin Pudding

Per serving: 185 Calories, 780 Kilojoules, 2g Protein, 5g Fat, 33g Carbohydrate, 3g Fibre, 10mg Sodium

Serves 4-6
225-350g (8-10oz) brown short-grain rice, washed and drained
1 litre (1$\frac{3}{4}$ pints) milk
1 strip of thinly pared lemon rind
100g (4oz) seedless raisins
6 tablespoons clear honey
1 teaspoon rose water
2 tablespoons dark rum (optional)
50g (2oz) blanched almonds, toasted

Preparation time: 10 minutes
Cooking time: 50 minutes

1. Put the rice and the milk into a saucepan with the strip of lemon rind. Bring slowly to the boil, stirring occasionally, and simmer very gently for about 40 minutes or until the rice is tender and has absorbed the milk.
2. Stir in the raisins, honey and rose water and simmer for 5 minutes. Discard the lemon rind, stir in the rum and set aside to cool slightly. Pour the rice into a serving dish and, when it is cold, scatter the almonds on top.

Sticky Fruitbread

Per average slice: 156 Calories, 650 Kilojoules, 3g Protein, 2g Fat, 34g Carbohydrate, 3g Fibre, 25mg Sodium

Makes two 450g (1lb) loaves
3 tablespoons malt extract
2 tablespoons molasses
25g (1oz) soft margarine
450g (1lb) wholewheat flour
salt
1 teaspoon ground cinnamon
225g (8oz) sultanas
15g ($\frac{1}{2}$oz) instant dried yeast
150ml ($\frac{1}{4}$ pint) water
Glaze:
1 tablespoon muscovado sugar
1 tablespoon water
1 tablespoon skimmed milk

Preparation time: 25 minutes, plus standing
Cooking time: 40 minutes
Oven: 200°C, 400°F, Gas Mark 6

1. Heat a tablespoon and measure the malt extract and molasses into a small saucepan. Add the margarine and heat gently until all the ingredients have melted. Stir to blend them thoroughly. Cool slightly.
2. Sift the flour, salt and cinnamon into a mixing bowl, tip in any bran remaining in the sieve and stir in the sultanas and yeast. Pour the cooled malt mixture and the water on to the dry ingredients and quickly mix to a soft dough. Lightly knead the dough until it is smooth.
3. Divide the dough into 2 equal pieces and press them into 2 greased 450g (1lb) loaf tins. Cover the tins with greased polythene and stand them in a warm place for about 1 hour or until the dough has risen to the top of the tins.
4. Bake the loaves in a preheated oven for 35 minutes until they are cooked. The loaves should sound hollow when tapped underneath.
5. Place the glaze ingredients in a small saucepan and stir over low heat until the sugar has dissolved, then boil for 1 minute. Brush the glaze over the hot loaves. Stand the tins on a wire rack to cool. Ⓐ
Ⓐ Wrap the fruitbread in foil and store in an airtight tin for up to 2 weeks.

Figgy Scone Bread

Per piece: 200 Calories, **820** Kilojoules, 5g Protein, 7g Fat, 33g Carbohydrate, 5g Fibre, 145mg Sodium

Makes one 20cm (8 inch) round scone
175g (6oz) wholewheat flour
1 teaspoon baking powder
salt
25g (1oz) light muscovado sugar
50g (2oz) fine oatmeal
75g (3oz) soft margarine
100g (4oz) dried figs, finely chopped
about 150ml ($\frac{1}{4}$ pint) skimmed milk
2 tablespoons clear honey, melted

Preparation time: 20 minutes
Cooking time: 25 minutes
Oven: 200°C, 400°F, Gas Mark 6

1. Sift the flour, baking powder and salt into a mixing bowl, tip in any bran remaining in the sieve and stir in the sugar and oatmeal. Using a fork, beat in the margarine and stir in the figs and just enough milk to form a soft dough. Knead the dough lightly until it is smooth.
2. Press the dough into a greased 20cm (8 inch) round tin and mark into 6 wedges. Brush the top with honey.
3. Bake in a preheated oven for 25 minutes, or until the scone is well risen and golden brown. Cool the scone partly in the tin, then turn it out on to a wire rack. Serve this bread warm if possible; it is specially good with cottage cheese.

Clockwise from the left: Figgy scone bread; Oaty drop scones with cherry sauce; Apricot and ginger scone bars

Prune and Nut Teabread

Per piece: 190 Calories, **800** Kilojoules, 6g Protein, 9g Fat, 32g Carbohydrate, 5g Fibre, 45mg Sodium

Makes on 15cm (6 inch) round loaf
225g (8oz) wholewheat self-raising flour
salt
pinch of grated nutmeg
$\frac{1}{4}$ teaspoon ground allspice
1 teaspoon grated orange rind
25g (1oz) soft margarine
75g (3oz) chopped walnuts
75g (3oz) prunes, stoned and chopped
1 egg
100ml (3$\frac{1}{2}$fl oz) buttermilk or skimmed milk
3 tablespoons orange juice

Preparation time: 15 minutes
Cooking time: 45 minutes
Oven: 190°C, 375°F, Gas Mark 5

1. Sift the flour, salt, nutmeg and allspice into a mixing bowl, tip in any bran remaining in the sieve and stir in the orange rind. Rub in the margarine, using a fork. Stir in the walnuts and prunes. Beat the egg with the buttermilk or milk and the orange juice. Pour on to the dry ingredients and mix quickly to form a stiff batter.
2. Turn the mixture into a greased 15cm (6 inch) round cake tin.
3. Bake in a preheated oven for 40-45 minutes or until the teabread is well risen and golden brown and a fine skewer pierced through the centre comes out clean. Stand the tin on a wire rack to cool, then turn out the teabread and allow to become cold. Ⓐ Serve spread with sieved cottage cheese and honey.

Ⓐ The teabread will store well for 3-4 days. Closely wrap it in foil and store in an airtight tin.

1. Sift the flour, soda, 1 teaspoon of the ginger, the mixed spice and salt into a mixing bowl and tip in the bran remaining in the sieve. Using a fork beat in the soft margarine and stir in the apricots. Stir in the yogurt and mix to form a ball. Knead the dough lightly until it is smooth.

2. Press the dough into a greased 18cm (7 inch) square baking tin. Brush the top with milk, sprinkle on the sugar mixed with the remaining ginger and mark the top into bars.

3. Bake the scone in a preheated oven for 25 minutes, until it is well risen and firm. Cool slightly in the tin, then transfer it to a wire rack. Cut into bars and serve warm.

Oaty Drop Scones with Cherry Sauce

Per scone: 85 Calories, 350 Kilojoules, 3g Protein, 2g Fat, 16g Carbohydrate, 2g Fibre, 130mg Sodium

Makes about 30 scones
75g (3oz) wholewheat self-raising flour
2 teaspoons baking powder
salt
40g (1½oz) medium oatmeal
1 egg, lightly beaten
2 tablespoons clear honey
150ml (¼ pint) plain unsweetened yogurt
oil, for greasing (optional)
plain unsweetened yogurt, to serve
Sauce:
225g (8oz) dessert cherries, stoned
2 tablespoons bramble jelly
1 tablespoon lemon juice
1 tablespoon water

Preparation time: 20 minutes
Cooking time: 25 minutes

1. Sift the flour, baking powder and salt into a mixing bowl and tip in any bran remaining in the sieve. Stir in the oatmeal, then beat in the egg, honey and yogurt. Beat to make a smooth batter.

2. Heat a heavy frying pan or a griddle and brush it lightly with oil if necessary. Drop 2 teaspoons of the batter, well apart, on to the heated surface and cook for about 3 minutes until the tops start to bubble. Flip the scones over with a palette knife and cook the other side for 2-3 minutes. Keep the scones warm in a folded tea-towel while you cook the rest of the batter in the same way.

3. To make the sauce, put the cherries, jelly, lemon juice and water into a saucepan, stir over low heat until the jelly has melted, then bring to the boil. Simmer for 5 minutes until the cherry juice runs. Stir well. Ⓐ Serve the scones warm, with the hot sauce and yogurt separately.

Ⓐ Make the sauce 1 day ahead, refrigerate and serve cold.

Apricot and Ginger Scone Bars

Per piece: 195 Calories, 815 Kilojoules, 4g Protein, 2g Fat, 20g Carbohydrate, 6g Fibre, 140mg Sodium

Makes one 18cm (7 inch) square scone
225g (8oz) wholewheat flour
1 teaspoon bicarbonate of soda
1½ teaspoons ground ginger
pinch of mixed ground spice
salt
75g (3oz) soft margarine
100g (4oz) dried apricot pieces, chopped
150ml (¼ pint) plain unsweetened yogurt
2 tablespoons milk, for brushing
2 tablespoons demerara sugar

Preparation time: 15 minutes
Cooking time: 25 minutes
Oven: 220°C, 425°F, Gas Mark 7

Semolina Singing Hinny

Per scone 170 Calories, 700 Kilojoules, 6g Protein, 3g fat, 32g Carbohydrate, 4g Fibre, 80mg Sodium

Makes 12 scones
350g (12oz) wholewheat self-raising flour
1 teaspoon baking powder
salt
100g (4oz) wholewheat semolina
25g (1oz) soft margarine
25g (1oz) light muscovado sugar
75g (3oz) currants
150ml ($\frac{1}{4}$ pint) skimmed milk
150ml ($\frac{1}{4}$ pint) plain unsweetened yogurt
oil, for brushing (optional)

Preparation time: 15 minutes
Cooking time: 20 minutes

1. Sift the flour, baking powder and salt into a mixing bowl and stir in the semolina. Using a fork beat in the soft margarine and stir in the sugar and currants. Pour on the milk and yogurt and quickly mix to form a firm dough. Knead the dough lightly until it is smooth.
2. Roll out the dough on a lightly floured board to make two 20cm (8 inch) rounds. Prick the tops all over with a fork and cut each round into 6 wedges.
3. Heat a heavy-based frying pan or a griddle and brush it with oil if necessary. Cook the scones over moderately high heat for 3-4 minutes on each side. Serve warm.

Orange Marmalade Ring

Per piece (of 10) 310 Calories, 1290 Kilojoules, 4g Protein, 19g Fat, 32g Carbohydrate, 4g Fibre, 130mg Sodium

Makes one 23cm (9 inch) ring cake
225g (8oz) wholewheat flour
salt
2 teaspoons baking powder
1 teaspoon ground cinnamon
50g (2oz) light muscovado sugar
8 tablespoons low-sugar orange marmalade, chopped
grated rind and juice of 1 orange
175ml (6fl oz) vegetable oil
2 eggs
150g (5oz) seedless raisins
2 tablespoons honey, melted, to glaze

Preparation time: 20 minutes
Cooking time: 1 hour 5 minutes
Oven: 160°C, 325°F, Gas Mark 3

1. Sift the flour, salt, baking powder and cinnamon into a bowl and tip in any bran remaining in the sieve. In another bowl mix together the sugar, marmalade, orange rind, reserving some strands for decoration, orange juice and oil and beat in the eggs. Gradually beat in the flour mixture, and stir in the raisins.
2. Turn the mixture into a greased and floured 23cm (9 inch) metal ring mould.
3. Bake in a preheated oven for 1 hour and 5 minutes, or until the cake is well risen and firm.
4. Leave the cake to cool a little in the ring, then turn it out on to a wire tray. Brush it with the melted honey while it is still warm. Cool the cake completely, then wrap it in foil. Ⓐ Decorate with the remaining strands.
Ⓐ This cake will store well in an airtight tin for up to 1 week, and is anyway best left to mature for 1-2 days.

Crunchy Muesli Bars

Per bar: 165 Calories, 690 Kilojoules, 3g Protein, 10g Fat, 18g Carbohydrate, 3g Fibre, 10mg Sodium

Makes one 28 × 18cm (11 × 7 inch) slab
4 tablespoons vegetable oil
6 tablespoons honey
25g (1oz) light muscovado sugar
150g (6oz) porridge oats
50g (2oz) sunflower seeds
25g (1oz) sesame seeds
25g (1oz) desiccated coconut
50g (2oz) dried apricot pieces, chopped
50g (2oz) sultanas

Preparation time: 10 minutes
Cooking time: 20-25 minutes
Oven: 180°C, 350°F, Gas Mark 4

1. Put the oil and the honey into a saucepan and heat gently until the honey has melted. Remove from the heat and stir in all the remaining ingredients.
2. Press the mixture into a greased 28 × 18cm (11 × 7 inch) baking tin and level the top.
3. Bake in a preheated oven for 20-25 minutes until the biscuit is golden brown. Mark it into bars while it is still hot. Cool slightly, then cut into slices. Remove them from the tin and cool on a wire rack. Ⓐ
Ⓐ Store the bars in an airtight tin. They will keep for 1 week.

Clockwise from the left: Orange marmalade ring;
Honey and hazelnut teacakes; Crunchy muesli bars

Honey and Hazelnut Teacakes

Per teacake: 300 Calories, 1250 Kilojoules, 10g Protein, 10g Fat, 45g Carbohydrate, 6g Fibre, 70mg Sodium

Makes 8 scones
100g (4oz) wholewheat flour
1 teaspoon light muscovado sugar
1 tablespoon dried yeast
175ml (6fl oz) tepid skimmed milk
Dough:
350g (12fl oz) wholewheat flour
salt
50g (2oz) soft margarine
3 tablespoons clear honey, melted
75g (3oz) chopped hazelnuts
1 egg, beaten
Glaze:
1 tablespoon light muscovado sugar
1 tablespoon skimmed milk

Preparation time: 30 minutes, plus standing and rising
Cooking time: 25 minutes
Oven: 220°C, 425°F, Gas Mark 7

1. Mix together the flour, sugar and dried yeast, pour on the milk and mix to a smooth batter. Set aside in a warm place for about 15 minutes until the mixture is frothy.
2. To make the dough, sift the flour and salt in a mixing bowl, rub in the margarine, using a fork, and stir in the honey, nuts and egg. Pour on the yeast batter mixture and mix until the dough leaves the sides of the bowl.
3. Turn out the dough on to a lightly floured board and knead for about 10 minutes, or until it is smooth and pliable. (Use the dough hook attachment of your mixer to save time.) Shape the dough into a ball, return it to the bowl and cover with a piece of oiled polythene. Leave it in a warm place for about 45 minutes, or until it has doubled in size.
4. Knead the dough lightly and divide it into 8 equal pieces. Shape the dough into rounds and place them well apart on 2 baking sheets.
5. Bake the teacakes in a preheated oven for 20 minutes, or until they sound hollow when tapped underneath. Mix together the milk and sugar for the glaze, brush it over the teacakes and return them to the oven for 2-3 minutes. Serve warm, split and filled with honey and low-fat soft cheese, or split and toasted.

Index